COUPLES COMMUNICATION
Workbook

26 Practices for Resolving Conflict,
Having Constructive Discussions,
and Building Strong Connection
and Deeper Intimacy

Written by
Myranda Thrussell

Table of Contents

Introduction

Love relationships bring wonderful and unforgettable moments, but it's natural to face and overcome challenging phases together. It's common for healthy couples to experience relationship issues and seek couples counseling, either in person or online. Often, concerns are directly or indirectly related to communication challenges within the couple, and if unaddressed, they can lead to significant relationship discomfort. Learning to communicate effectively and improving these skills can make a significant difference in your relationship. Couples can use effective communication activities to discover how to strengthen their love bond.

In this workbook, you will learn about the importance of relationship communication practices and explore various communication activities to help you connect with your partner on a deeper level. Couples therapy communication activities teach couples how to communicate and respond to each other effectively. This constructive communication approach includes sharing thoughts, information, ideas, and knowledge productively. How well you communicate directly impacts how well you can work together as a team. Solid communication can enhance intimacy and reaffirm trust in your partner.

Evidence shows that couples achieve greater intimacy through countless everyday activities and situations where they intentionally cultivate emotional connections. Emotional connection skills are crucial for strong couples, making it an essential part of their relationship toolkit. Communication involves engaging with another person by exchanging information or resources and, in some cases, seeking support or comfort. Communication can create a connection when one person understands certain concepts from the other, even through nonverbal cues.

Human beings use both verbal and nonverbal methods in communication, governed by several complex rules. Emotional and paralinguistic markers are just some of the symbols people use to interact with each other in daily encounters. Communication is a two-way street, and the way it's spoken significantly impacts how it's received. Nonverbal communication between spouses, such as body language, gestures, facial expressions, and eye contact, plays a significant role in how they perceive and interact with each other.

Through engaging in communication activities, couples learn to communicate courteously and effectively. While the exercises focus on specific skill sets, they aim to re-establish deeper trust and connection. This practical guide contains essential self-analysis exercises for working on verbal and non-verbal communication.

Chapter 1: Why Is Communication the Key to a Lasting Relationship?

Communication is crucial for human interaction and personal relationships, as it allows us to gain insight into another person's thoughts and feelings. Research on married couples has shown that emotional connection is the most critical factor in determining relationship quality and whether a couple perceives their marriage as successful. Intimate communication involves more than just exchanging words; it also includes building an emotional bond.

There are some typical differences in communication styles between women and men, as observed by sociolinguistics researchers. These gender differences, however, don't apply to everyone. Women tend to use words more than men to express themselves and are more likely to provide and receive support from others with intensive eye contact and vocal encouragement. Studies suggest that men may withdraw when overstimulated by this type of communication. Marriage counselors have begun to explore the importance of these differences for improving marital relationships.

1.1 Emotional Communication

Emotional communication is the heart and lungs of a relationship, creating a meaningful connection between two people. This type of communication allows ideas and feelings to be shared and involves paying attention to one another. What matters most in effective communication is how individuals interact with each other, not necessarily the content of their discussions or their level of agreement.

1.2 Strategies for Successful Connection

To improve a couple's relationship through better communication, several factors contribute to effective communication. These include:

- **Being clear**: Clear expression of underlying desires for connection leads to more favorable outcomes.

- **Being nice**: Partners who can speak softly and use humor and playfulness are more likely to build lasting, high-quality relationships.

- **Being caring**: Both parties need to feel cared for and validated to have a healthy relationship.

- **Staying positive**: Most positive contact is essential for engaging rather than isolating or alienating communication.

1.3 Open Communication Connects People

Open communication, characterized by honesty, vulnerability, and mutual influence, helps partners create a positive foundation for their relationship. Successfully intimate couples can express their emotions and opinions, even if they differ from their partner's, and engage in conversations that deepen their understanding of each other.

Sharing power in a relationship is also linked to openness. Men who are more receptive to their wives' opinions tend to have happier and more stable relationships. For partners to feel welcome and understood, they need to cultivate mutual influence or be comfortable in their relationship.

1.4 Mastering Conflict: Building a Resilient Relationship

Conflict is not an enemy to relationships; rather, it can be a sign of healthy engagement. It's not about the frequency of disagreements, but how partners handle and resolve them. In managing conflict, couples should embrace open communication, maintain a positive tone, and strive to understand each other better. This approach can facilitate personal growth and deepen relationships.

However, there are toxic patterns that can undermine these efforts: rapid escalation of conflict, avoidance or withdrawal, negative interpretations, and verbal attacks or put-downs. These patterns distort communication and can quickly erode the emotional connection between partners.

Here are the harmful patterns to watch out for:

1. **Escalation**: Disagreements that rapidly become more intense and hostile. De-escalation techniques like lowering voice pitch, empathizing with the other person, and taking timeouts can be beneficial.

2. **Withdrawal or Avoidance**: When one partner avoids engaging in a discussion or conflict, it may lead to feelings of abandonment in the other partner. Balance can be achieved if both partners make a conscious effort to engage, even when it's uncomfortable.

3. **Negative Interpretations**: When partners primarily focus on the negatives, it often results in hostile responses and further conflict. Making a conscious effort to interpret actions positively can mitigate this.

4. **Put-Downs**: Insults and disrespectful comments erode the emotional connection and can result in relationship breakdown. It's vital to take a moment to calm down and think before making such remarks.

1.5 The Art of Teaching Effective Communication to Couples

Teaching couples to communicate effectively is an ongoing process. While short communication workshops or miracle solutions can't transform a relationship overnight, they can plant the seeds of understanding and motivate couples to continue learning.

Recognizing signs of an unhealthy relationship is crucial, including persistent negativity, verbal abuse, severe criticism, or defensive behavior. Just as people seek medical help for physical symptoms, couples should seek professional advice when their relationship shows signs of distress. Education should prioritize emotional and physical safety and promote the development of emotional communication skills as the foundation of a strong, connected relationship.

As a side note, in the case of abusive or harmful relationships, professional help should be sought immediately, and continuation of such relationships should never be advocated.

Chapter 2: Our Body Communicates Even Without Speaking

Our body language, including posture, facial expressions, gestures, and voice inflections, plays a significant role in conveying information. Understanding and utilizing body language can enhance personal and professional relationships.

2.1 What Is Body Language?

Body language is the nonverbal representation of thoughts and feelings through physical movements, often done spontaneously rather than intentionally. Even when you're silent, your body continuously communicates non-verbal messages that others may interpret as an indication of your thoughts or emotions. Consistency between your spoken words and body language is crucial for building trust and connection with others.

2.2 The Importance of Nonverbal Communication

Nonverbal communication signals, such as facial expressions, gestures, posture, and eye contact, convey emotions and intentions more effectively than words alone. Being aware of your body language and nonverbal cues, as well as those of others, can expand your communication skills and foster deeper connections.

2.3 Types of Nonverbal Communication

Body language or nonverbal communication includes a wide range of techniques, such as:

Facial expressions. A person's face is a powerful tool for conveying a wide range of emotions without expressing a single word. When it comes to facial expressions, they are universally recognized. Across nations, the facial emotions of joy, sorrow, rage, shock, terror, and contempt are alike.

Body movement and posture. Consider how the way someone walks, the posture they assume, sits, or how they look at you quickly affects your impression of them. The way you behave and move tells the world around you who you are, what you think and how you feel. There is a wide range of nonverbal communication techniques that may be used to convey your personality.

Gestures. Throughout the day, you use gestures to express yourselves. When arguing or speaking excitedly, you might communicate without considering by waving, pointing, calling, or using your hands. However, some gestures can take on different, or even opposite, meanings, depending on the cultural context in which they are used. For example, making the "OK" gesture with the hand is a positive sign in English-speaking nations, while it is given offensive meaning in countries like Brazil, Russia, and Germany. It is therefore essential to pay attention when using gestures to avoid misunderstandings that can compromise communication with the person in front of us.

Eye contact. This is a particularly meaningful non-verbal communication, as many individuals rely heavily on the visual sense. The way you stare at your partner can convey various emotions, such as love, hate, jealousy, anger, etc. Note the other person's interest and reaction as you make eye contact to move the discussion forward.

Touch. Touch is a major part of how people communicate. It's important to remember that even a feeble handshake, a kind pat on the head, or an affectionate bear hug sends various meanings.

Space. Have you felt the other people were encroaching on your personal space during a discussion? Even while your needs for physical space vary based on your cultural and personal contexts, you all have a basic need for it. Many nonverbal messages may be sent via physical space, such as signs of closeness, love, hostility, or dominance.

Voice. In addition to what you say, how you express it is as essential. In addition to hearing what you say, others may "read" your voice as you talk. Timing and tempo, volume, intonation, and noises that suggest awareness, such as "ahh" and "uh-huh," are all elements they pay close attention to. Reflect on the many ways your voice tone might convey various emotions.

2.4 Can Nonverbal Communication Be Faked?

Although it is possible to learn specific body language techniques to appear more confident or dominant, such strategies may not always be successful. Instead of trying to fake nonverbal cues, focus on being genuine and open-minded, which will lead to more authentic and effective communication.

2.5 How Can Nonverbal Communication Go Wrong?

Miscommunication can occur when people are unaware of the ambiguous or negative nonverbal messages they are sending. This can damage trust and connection in relationships. To avoid misunderstandings, it is essential to develop self-awareness and improve nonverbal communication skills.

2.6 How to Improve Nonverbal Communication?

Improving nonverbal communication involves being fully present, managing stress, and increasing emotional awareness. By focusing on these aspects, you can better understand and respond to the nonverbal cues of others.

2.6.1 Be Fully Present

To effectively pick up on nonverbal cues, it's essential to be completely focused on the conversation at hand. This means avoiding distractions like checking your phone or planning what you're going to say next. By being fully present, you're more likely to notice and understand the nonverbal signals being sent by your conversation partner.

2.6.2 Develop Your Emotional Awareness

Stress can have a negative impact on your communication skills, making it more difficult to accurately interpret and convey nonverbal messages. It's important to recognize when you're feeling stressed and take steps to manage it. Techniques such as deep breathing, mindfulness, and meditation can help you regain your emotional balance and improve your ability to communicate effectively.

2.6.3 Learn to Manage Stress

Emotional awareness is crucial for effective nonverbal communication. It involves recognizing and understanding your emotions as well as the emotions of others. By developing your emotional awareness, you can:

• Empathize with others by accurately interpreting their thoughts, feelings, and nonverbal cues.

13

• Build trust in relationships by ensuring your verbal and nonverbal messages are consistent.

• Communicate in a way that demonstrates active listening and genuine care for the other person.

Practicing mindfulness and self-reflection can help you cultivate greater emotional awareness.

2.7 How to Read Body Language?

As you improve your stress management and emotional awareness, you'll become better at detecting nonverbal cues from others. To read body language effectively, keep the following in mind:

• Look for inconsistencies between verbal and nonverbal messages.

• Examine nonverbal signals as a group, rather than focusing on a single gesture.

• Trust your intuition when it comes to detecting dishonesty or inconsistencies.

By paying attention to factors like eye contact, facial expressions, tone of voice, posture, and gestures, you can gain a more profound understanding of what someone is truly feeling or thinking.

2.8 Body Language Tips to Strengthen Your Relationship

Effective body language can have a positive impact on your relationship. Here are some tips to help you improve your nonverbal communication with your partner:

• Slow down when apologizing or resolving conflicts, as this can help convey sincerity.

• Offer nice touches or hugs when your partner is feeling stressed or upset, as this can provide comfort and support.

• Keeping steady eye contact communicates that you are fully involved and attentively listening to the dialogue.

• Learn to read your partner's body language to better understand their emotions and thoughts.

By focusing on these aspects of nonverbal communication, you can strengthen your relationship and foster a deeper connection with your partner.

Chapter 3: Enhancing Communication through Emotional Intelligence

As our society evolves, we become more efficient, better informed, and ostensibly "smarter". Our perception of success often hinges on the count of people we supersede or outpace. However, this advancement often overlooks a fundamental element of human connection. With mental health concerns on the rise and traditional social ties diminishing, it's clear something is missing.

In this chapter, we delve into how modern history has reshaped society's understanding of connectedness.

3.1 Emotional Intelligence (EI) and Social Skills

As psychologists recognized multiple distinct types of intelligence that couldn't be measured on a linear scale, theories of intelligence expanded. The emphasis on traditional intelligence as an indicator of success was deemed exaggerated and unreliable. This realization came to the fore when researchers found that individuals with average IQs typically outperformed those with the highest IQs.

New metrics like "emotional quotient" and "social quotient" (SQ) emerged to measure these different skill sets alongside the conventional "intelligence quotient" (IQ). As Matthews, Zeidner, and Roberts (2004) suggest, emotional intelligence has gained global attention since its inception due to the importance modern society places on emotional management.

In this section, we will explore the contemporary significance of emotional intelligence and contrast it with other interpersonal skills such as social awareness, social intelligence, and empathy. While these skills may seem alike, they are actually quite distinct.

To give a concrete example of emotional intelligence in action, we will dedicate an entire section to its role in fostering healthy, long-lasting relationships among couples.

3.2 The Importance of Emotional Intelligence in Couples Communication

As our society continually evolves, we are becoming more informed and "intelligent" in its complex definition. We measure success by how many individuals we can surpass. Despite these advancements, the essential aspects of social connections are becoming eclipsed. Mental health issues are rising, and traditional community ties are weakening. In this section, we will explore how the evolution of society has shaped our understanding of connection and relatedness.

As the understanding of intelligence expanded, theories of intelligence became more comprehensive. This shift happened for two reasons: traditional intelligence was seen as overrated and not the sole predictor of success. Moreover, researchers discovered that individuals with average IQs often outperformed those with high IQs. As a result, new metrics like "emotional quotient" (EQ) and "social quotient" (SQ) emerged to quantify these different skills.

Emotional intelligence (EQ) is a key determinant of successful, long-lasting relationships. By enhancing your EQ, you can attract the empathetic partner you've been seeking and identify subtle shifts in your relationship that require your attention. This chapter will delve into how your EQ can elevate your romantic relationships and how to improve your connection with your partner.

3.2.1 Emotionally Intelligent Romantic Partnerships

High EQ skills are crucial in avoiding common relationship pitfalls such as mistaking infatuation for long-term love or letting unaddressed feelings jeopardize the relationship. Even if your EQ isn't at its peak when you begin a relationship, the experience of falling in love can motivate you to improve.

3.2.2 Strengthening Your Connection

Positive change in a relationship doesn't have to be feared. In fact, intentional changes can significantly strengthen your relationship. Relationships are dynamic, and change is inevitable. Embracing change provides you with confidence and optimism for the future.

As a practical exercise, create a list of at least five things your partner may need from you right now. What is the first action you will take tomorrow to start meeting these needs? Reflecting on these questions will help you stay connected with your partner and maintain a thriving relationship.

....

....

....

....

....

....

....

....

....

3.2.3 Transforming Challenges into Opportunities

In relationships fueled by resilience and optimism, difficulties aren't seen as stumbling blocks but rather opportunities for growth. What new understandings can both of you gain? With an acute awareness of your emotions, you can avoid the trappings of repeating past mistakes fueled by negative feelings. High emotional intelligence frees you from recurring patterns and rigidity, allowing you to innovate solutions to problems. Differences and inevitable discord can be seen as chances to understand each other better, challenges that can bring you closer, and tests that can make you emerge stronger as a team.

3.2.4 Embracing Each Other's Feelings

Loving someone doesn't mean that you will always delight in their actions; sometimes, you will be disappointed, angered, or hurt by your partner's behaviors. The key is not to ignore these feelings, but to experience them fully and choose how to respond. Blame has harmed many relationships, and guilt has prevented countless couples from experiencing true intimacy. Behind these harmful sentiments often lie unresolved anger, fear, and sadness. With a high level of emotional intelligence, you can voice these feelings, cope with them, and move forward in your relationship.

3.2.5 Keeping a Sense of Humor in Your Relationship

Laughter is a crucial element of acceptance; it is essential not to over-analyze your feelings. Couples who can't laugh at their foibles typically feel insecure about their relationship. They're likely less tolerant of their relationship's flaws and missteps, just as they are with their own, limiting their ability to appreciate the best aspects of being together. With high emotional intelligence, you can continuously strengthen your relationship without being burdened by unrealistic standards of perfection.

3.2.6 Observing Your Feelings When Your Partner Isn't Present

Fortunately, you have an accurate way to gauge your relationship's health: check in with your emotional, physical, and social well-being. Apart from feeling stressed or irritated, how are you faring emotionally? Do you feel lethargic at work or school following an evening of marital bliss? Despite spending quality time together, do you feel resentment toward your loved ones? Tunnel vision in love isn't beneficial. Regardless of how affectionate you are as a couple, it won't matter unless you feel energized, clear-headed, and compassionate consistently. If, for example, you're struggling to get out of bed in the morning despite having enjoyable intimacy with your partner the night before, something is off. When this happens, the insights you've gained about yourself, your partner, and your relationship should guide you towards the best resolution.

3.3 Social Intelligence vs. Emotional Intelligence

A 'one size fits all' approach doesn't apply when discussing interpersonal dynamics, given the myriad of variables involved. The deeper we delve into the realm of psychology, the easier it becomes to pinpoint specific areas where we need to enrich our lives. It's crucial to distinguish between social and emotional intelligence; while closely intertwined, they correspond to two disparate sets of social skills.

Emotional intelligence, in essence, is an amalgamation of emotional awareness and cognitive comprehension that enables individuals to understand themselves and others better.

Conversely, being "socially aware" involves understanding how global social, political, and economic divides influence our daily lives, the lives of our loved ones, neighbors, and even strangers we may never encounter. When enacted, social awareness appears to be a blend of empathy and familiarity with diverse social realities. 'Street smarts,' a related concept, is deemed a form of intelligence that results more from upbringing than nature (i.e., genetics).

Exposure to a wide array of social experiences cultivates understanding that shapes one's ability to interpret and navigate their social environment. Riggio (2014) identifies various attributes that characterize socially intelligent individuals:

- They exhibit enthusiasm, articulate fluency, and the capacity to easily engage in conversations with diverse individuals. They are flexible and adaptable in social situations. Often, these individuals relish being the center of attention at parties or large gatherings.

- They possess a profound comprehension of social norms. As a result, they can seamlessly switch between social roles to align with others' expectations, an act they perform with grace and conviction.

- They demonstrate exceptional listening skills, going beyond merely hearing to truly understanding and focusing on another person's words. This ability to fully immerse themselves in another person's perspective is rare, as most people are primarily preoccupied with their thoughts (i.e., worldview). Such individuals are lauded socially for their acute self-awareness, fostering trust and empathy.

- They have the capability to observe, empathize, and reason. Social Intelligence involves getting to know a person on an emotional level and being aware of the overall 'vibe' they are emitting. This constitutes the emotional aspect of Social Intelligence. It also requires the ability to discern what the other person is thinking and interpret their body language. Individuals with high Social Intelligence realize that how they present themselves affects how others perceive them. Thus, if they aim to leave a positive first impression, they would go to great lengths to look their best and behave courteously.

3.4 Getting to Know "the Right One"

How do you determine whether the person you're falling in love with is "the one" when you're just starting to feel those feelings? How can one tell the difference between falling in love with a real person and falling in love with love itself? If you've been hurt in the past, how can you protect yourself from making the same errors again?

3.4.1 Prioritizing Feelings Over Thoughts

Often, we choose life partners based more on our cognitions and beliefs rather than our emotions. Our interactions are dictated by what we perceive things ought to be or should have been. This is precisely where our mental judgement falters. In matters of love, our failures don't stem from letting our emotions overwhelm us, but rather, letting our thoughts dominate.

People might believe they're in love for a range of reasons, including passion, infatuation, the desire for security, prestige, societal approval, and so on. They may feel they've discovered true love, simply because a potential partner fits a particular image or standard. However, until they truly connect with their feelings, their decision is likely to falter.

When your daydreams about a potential love interest begin to morph into internal dialogues that rationalize your choices or cause you to stress over them, it's a good time to pause. Take deep breaths, attempt to relax, and focus on something else. This helps to shift your awareness from your mind to your body. Suppose an intuition that something isn't quite right persists or grows stronger over time, this might suggest your decision was misjudged. By allowing cerebral notions rather than actual sensations to guide your decisions, you may never truly discover what you genuinely desire.

3.4.2 Pay Attention to What Your Whole Body Is Trying to Tell You

It is difficult for most individuals to acquire clear messages from their entire body at the beginning stages of a new romantic relationship, since they are often drowned out by sexual desire. Because of this, it is essential to be aware of other emotions that are subtler. If you are experiencing symptoms such as muscle tension, headaches, stomach problems, or a lack of energy, what you might want is not what you need. If, on the other hand, this feeling of love is accompanied by an increase in liveliness and energy, then this can be interpreted as a positive message that your body is sending you. If it's more than an infatuation or desire, you'll find that it improves other aspects of your life, as well as the connections you have with other people.

Put the following high EQ questions to yourself:

1. Is this partnership bringing new vitality into every aspect of my existence? Take my word as an example: has it become better? Am I trying to improve the way I look after myself?

2. Have I managed to get my bearings? Am I abler to concentrate, as well as be more creative and responsible?

3. Do my sentiments of "love" extend farther than just having a nice, caring attitude

toward my beloved? Do I have a greater sense of generosity, giving, and empathy while interacting with close friends, colleagues, or complete strangers?

If the responses you receive from your body aren't what you were hoping to hear, try to go over the normal dread of loss that we all feel at some point in our lives. If you find out now that you haven't discovered real love, it might save you the misery of a pile of terrible emotional memories in the future. These memories can be a legacy that causes you to keep making the same errors, or can turn you off love entirely.

3.4.3 Taking the Risk to Connect

When we encounter someone new, our instinct is often to be on guard, and as a result, we unconsciously build barriers that prevent us from truly connecting. Opening up might feel intimidating, but it's crucial for assessing the potential for real love and distinguishing it from illusion.

Try to make the first move; when it feels most terrifying, consider laughing at yourself, sharing a personal secret, or expressing kindness to the other person. Does their response make you feel a rush of warmth and vitality? If so, you might have found a sensitive and kindred soul. If not, you might be dealing with someone with low emotional intelligence, and you'll need to decide how to interact with them moving forward.

3.4.4 What You Desire vs. What Is Essential for You to Feel Loved

Learn the difference between the things you urgently need in a partner and the things that would be nice to have before you start your search for "the one". The activity that is explained in the following paragraph might be of assistance.

Choose and rank in decreasing order the top five qualities or traits that are most essential to you in a potential romantic partner. Think, for example, of someone who has a sense of humor, is neat, empathetic, adventurous, caring, emotionally intelligent, physically fit, elegant in their expression and movement, selfless, protective, with a creative mind; other qualities could be a conversational person, insightful, affectionate, wealthy, respected by others, charismatic, maternal or paternal, spiritual and faithful.

As you think about each quality, ask yourself if it energizes you, whether it soothes you, and whether it gets your emotions stirred up. How would you rate each individual quality from 1 to 10 after reflecting on the sensations they arouse in you? Once this is done, he begins to classify and write in descending order the top five qualities that have received the highest score. A want is a transient or relatively shallow sensation, but a need is something that registers on a deeper level of feeling.

Repeat the exercise a few times to obtain a better grasp of the distinctions between the things you want and the things you feel you require in a romantic relationship. Does the person you believe to be the object of your affection satisfy these requirements?

....
....
....
....
....
....
....
....
....

3.4.5 Reacting to a Love Relationship with a Poor Emotional Intelligence

Each person is different and requires their time to grow their "emotional muscles". If you are ahead of the one you love, here are some strategies to react to low EQ conduct and poor listeners that require high emotional intelligence.

Please spend some time thinking about the emotions you want your spouse to experience, as well as the words you want them to hear. The message you want to convey may be misunderstood if you are not clear about what you want and why you want it.

Choose a moment when neither you nor your spouse will be hurried or distracted by other obligations. You may go for a stroll together or make plans to have breakfast or dinner together, but if you want them to recall what you spoke about, you should limit their use of alcohol.

If you want your spouse to know that anything is wrong with them, you should send them "I feel" messages that focus on your requirements. For instance, you may say something like, "I have this aversion to the smell of onions and garlic, so I wondered if you would be willing to clean your teeth before going into bed".

Repeat your partner's worries to them if they respond defensively to the emotion you've shared with them. For example, you may say, "You're concerned that if I accept this job, you and the kids will be ignored".

It would be best if you restated your "I feel" message, then listened once again, and continued this procedure as often as necessary until you are certain that your message has been received.

3.5 Top 10 Ways to Be an Intelligent Lover

Navigating the path of love can be challenging, especially for those new to emotional intelligence (EQ). To make your journey smoother, keep these top 10 suggestions in mind and apply them to your relationship:

1. Prioritize emotional, physical, and spiritual health: Your love decisions should positively impact all aspects of your well-being. If your relationship makes you feel more energetic, mentally clear, and loving in general, it likely has a strong foundation.

2. Be open and authentic: Share your thoughts and feelings with your partner. Expressing your emotions is crucial, as it forms the essence of who you are. Genuine love can only be experienced when you're true to yourself.

3. Listen with empathy: Tune into the emotions your partner is experiencing as they speak. This will help you understand their perspective and feelings better.

4. Offer emotional support and affection: Different people have different needs when it comes to support and affection. Let empathy guide you in understanding your partner's preferences and responding accordingly.

5. Ask questions: Love doesn't provide all the answers. Try to inquire about your partner's thoughts and feelings on various topics to foster deeper understanding and connection.

6. Invest time and effort in the relationship: Don't take your relationship for granted once you've found your soulmate. Relationships require ongoing attention and nurturing to grow and thrive.

7. Learn from your partner: Practice active awareness to avoid relying on assumptions from experiences. Your partner can teach you valuable lessons about love, communication, and growth.

8. Be mindful of emotionally charged memories: Past emotional wounds can be harmful when they resurface in your current relationship. Recognize and address these feelings to prevent them from negatively affecting your bond.

9. Embrace mistakes and learn from them: It's impossible to avoid mistakes in complex relationships, but they can become opportunities for growth if approached without guilt or shame. The real challenge lies in refusing to acknowledge and learn from errors.

10. Embrace change as an opportunity for growth: Adapting to change can be challenging, but also offers a chance to refresh and reinvigorate your relationship. Use change as a catalyst to deepen your connection and foster mutual development.

By following these top 10 ways to be an emotionally intelligent lover, you'll cultivate a healthier, more fulfilling relationship built on understanding, empathy, and growth.

Chapter 4: Navigating Emotions and Disputes

Often, the only means of settling a problem is the capacity to speak it out. The ability to "hear" what the other person is saying (and frequently what they aren't saying) to make people feel heard is one-half of the key to successful communication in a conflict scenario. You must also be able to express yourself properly to the other side so that they can hear and comprehend what you are trying to say and that they will be sympathetic to what you are trying to convey.

In conflict situations, effective communication reduces stress, creates trust, deepens connections, and helps individuals feel more at ease since they understand one another. However, it does not waver on critical issues.

Peacekeeping conflicts result from an escalating crisis or an intense level of tension. Keeping the peace frequently necessitates collaborating with people from different cultural backgrounds, which adds to the difficulty of building trust and fostering understanding.

4.1 Key Things to Learn

- Be aware of your communication skills and shortcomings in a conflict scenario and how you may improve.

- Learn to perceive things from other people's perspectives, and how critical it is to be mindful of your own during a fight.

- Schedule time each week to learn some techniques to control and reduce stress and to speak clearly.

- Acquire a rudimentary understanding of cultural nuances in communication.

4.2 Effective Communication

Building healthy relationships with friends, colleagues, and family depends on being able to express yourself clearly. Many individuals, however, find it difficult to communicate openly when confronted with difficult topics.

There are many various types of family structures and cultures in which people grow up. It is in these years that we develop our communication and interpersonal skills. What we see and experience as children has a lasting impact on us, both consciously and subconsciously. Regardless of how your relative spoke with one other, how they treated you, or whether they were absent, these early events leave a lasting impression on you. This affects the way you think, feel, communicate, perceive and react to the world around you.

In addition, we communicate nonverbally at all times, as well. We communicate with one another through making little changes to our bodies and faces, as well as by altering the electric currents in our heads and hearts. Our innermost thoughts and sentiments may be heard even when we aren't saying anything at all. This is one way you may detect someone's "vibe" when they enter a room: you feel the thoughts and emotions they are experiencing.

The likelihood of misunderstandings and conflict increases when individuals have diverse or similar but dysfunctional communication styles. When individuals don't work on expanding their communication skills to offset old, unhelpful behaviors, it may cause problems in their relationships.

Passive aggression, indirectness, withholding, and blame are some milder manifestations of dysfunction. When tensions rise, this might devolve into berating, humiliating, and calling each other names.

These issues can be avoided, but there are methods to do it. With practice, we may improve our communication and listening skills. Having a feeling of belonging, safety, and freedom of expression are all linked to a sense of being heard and understood. It's possible to strengthen your relationships and your overall well-being by developing better communication skills.

4.3 Emotional Inconsistencies/Conflicts

Conflict, misunderstandings, and unmet emotional demands can only hurt the peace of a relationship and the well-being of the two people involved, regardless of what definition of happiness one chooses to adhere to.

Being in a relationship necessitates the surrender of some of the egocentric beliefs that functioned for a person when they were single. As difficult as it may seem, the process of uniting two peoples in one place, fostering closeness, and a common vision for the future is one that almost always requires a long time of discussion, compromise, and sacrifice.

There may be a few conflicts along the road, but they always take place in a civilized manner, with each partner taking care not to damage the other with their words. For some couples, this process goes smoothly; there may be a few disagreements here and there.

Is this something you'd be interested in? If that's the case, you're in luck: for many, this transition period is characterized by nightmare-like tones, characterized by feelings of impotence, grief, and melancholy.

As a result of contemporary society's emphasis on competition and individualism, our romantic relationships have suffered. Because of the ease with which one may choose and dismiss partners, one can quickly judge the degree to which a potential partner can help one achieve one's goals and dreams.

Driven by the belief that our partner may not be enough, and better options might exist, we can quickly break bonds that today tend to be fleeting and short-lived.

As a result of this way of thinking, when we eventually find someone we love, we are unable to effectively deal with conflict, our strong emotions, and our need to be open and honest about whom we really are.

Even if we want the relationship to be unbreakable and never end, it appears that life may change so rapidly that a breakup is as good as a rupture.

As a result, we dress in iron-clad clothing to protect ourselves from being exposed and even abandoned in our bare bodies.

To get out of this situation, we can use those social skills that are intertwined with emotional intelligence that contribute to well-being, on an emotional level and in terms of connection with the partner.

To say that one can "manage" a love relationship is an understatement. When it comes to ensuring that both parties are content with the connection they have with one other, there are several unwritten and unsaid rules that must be adhered to achieve so.

4.4 Healthy Communication in the Face of Conflict

It's very difficult to completely avoid conflict in a relationship. The conflict itself is not to be considered the main problem, but it is the way in which it is managed that can unite or cause division between two people. Disagreements, misinterpretations, and misunderstandings may either lead to a breakdown in the relationship or lead to a better future.

An efficient flow of ideas and sentiments between individuals is a sign of healthy communication. People generally take turns speaking and listening in this kind of situation. To have good communication, both parties need to be invested in the process. As the dialogue progresses, both parties are aware of how they're behaving.

If you're the one speaking, you may show your presence and involvement by establishing eye contact or utilizing your body language. The listener is receptive to what the speaker is saying and does not cut them off at the end of a phrase or shift their attention elsewhere.

4.4.1 Vitality of Healthy Communication

Long-term relationships can only thrive if both parties can communicate clearly. According to one research, couples reported higher levels of happiness in their relationships when their communication was more efficient. Intimacy in a relationship may be enhanced via healthy communication.

Conflict resolution in most cases depends on the quality of communication between you and your partner. As long as both parties have healthy ways of communicating, it is easier to agree.

When dealing with a severe issue, you may need to be more direct if the other person isn't responding well to a more indirect approach. On the other side, a method focusing on love, forgiveness, and validation might be effective for daily relationship challenges. Understanding good communication and how to adapt your style to suit the occasion is essential to success.

4.4.2 The Art of Long-Distance Communication

The communication methods of couples in long-distance relationships and those in proximity were shown to vary significantly, according to one research. Relationships involving long-distance participants:

- The use of video calling, voice calls, and texting increased.

- They attached great importance to their partner being more receptive to phone calls and text messages.

- Increased frequent and responsive messaging resulted in more contentment in romantic relationships for the participants.

- When you are in a long-distance relationship, you both need to know that you can talk to one other.

If you're dealing with a long-distance issue, you may not want to type out all you're thinking in a text message. Eventually, this might lead to misunderstood messages and a lack of opportunity for your spouse to react. When compared to other means of communication, such as text or email, audio, and visual media may help provide an improved level of closeness.

Consider video or phone calls instead of texting for more in-depth conversations.

When you are talking on the phone with your lover, focus only on the conversation. To make the other person feel appreciated, you must be present and cherish your time together. Using a video call is the same as having a face-to-face chat. If your spouse is expressing something you would rather not hear, try not to hang up on them. Make a pact to listen to one another. It's OK if one of you takes a break and schedules a new time to resume the conversation.

However, don't abandon your spouse in the cold. Your long-distance partner may be wounded much more if you neglect your phone for a short period of time during a fight. Before you hang up, see if you can predict the next time you'll get a phone or video conversation.

4.5 Nonviolent Communication Exchanges

This technique for conflict communication was created by the Center for Nonviolent Communication and is aimed to de-escalate tension and conflict while enabling parties to speak effectively about their needs.

An essential aspect of NVC is that it recognizes the importance of sentiments in conflict situations. Conflict might be obscured by negative emotions like rage, frustration, insecurity, or fear. These feelings can be quite intense. The initial problem rapidly loses importance as the attention shifts to the conflict's emotional overtones.

Thanks to NVC, other parties may communicate and accept emotions while still focusing on the more important topics. If both sides of the disagreement practice it, it works flawlessly, but it is also useful if one person is communicating "violently."

4.5.1 How Does This Work?

When you talk, remember to always keep the following in mind:

1. "When I hear/see that you..."

Appreciate and strive to understand what the other side is trying to convey (they would feel heard).

2. "Then I feel..."

Recognize your feelings and express them. They're not listening to you and may be making you angry. How pleased are you that your concerns are being addressed?

3. "My need is to..."

To understand why you're involved in the issue and what you need to settle, be explicit about what you want. Keep repeating this.

4. "And my request is..."

There are many confrontations where individuals don't know what they want or how to get it from one another. Keep this to a few key points. An essential thing in your life is to try to express yourself free of blame or judgment.

4.6 A Tune for Peace

Things you might do every day to help maintain harmony in your life, your family, and your life partner:

- Make it a daily ritual to sit in silence and contemplate how you want to connect to yourself and your partner.

- Keep in mind that we are all created equal.

- Be as concerned about the well-being of others as you are about your own.

- Make sure you're not demanding anything when you ask someone to do something.

- Don't stress to your partner what you don't want them to do, but instead express what you like them to do.

- Instead of expressing your desire for someone to be a certain way, express what action you hope that person will do to assist that person in becoming that way.

- Before drawing conclusions, and agreeing or disagreeing, be attentive and sensitive to the feelings and needs of the person in front of you.

- Instead of saying "no," explain why you can't say "yes."

- Instead of blaming others or yourself when you're feeling down, focus on what you can do to address your needs.

- Express your appreciation by letting the person know that your need was met by thanking them instead of complimenting them.

Intense pressure is part of the job description on a peace mission. By daily meditating on a chosen mantra, you can manage daily stress better and boost productivity.

4.7 Resolving Conflicts Through Effective Communication

Avoid a negative result by using these suggestions for successful communication the next time you're faced with a quarrel. The following is an example of how to do it this way.

4.7.1 Keep Your Eyes on the Prize

When dealing with present issues, it's easy to bring up apparently relevant old problems. When you're already dealing with an issue, it may seem like a good idea to speak about all the things that are upsetting you at once.

But this method frequently obscures the issue, making it more difficult to come to an agreement on how to resolve the present issue. It might complicate the topic and possibly make it more difficult to understand. Try to avoid bringing up old wounds or other issues while you're speaking with someone. Do not lose sight of the fact that you are currently, your emotions, your mutual understanding, and finding a solution.

Mindfulness meditation may help you learn to be present in all aspects of your life, especially in the way you communicate with others.

4.7.2 Take Your Time and Pay Attention

When the other person stops talking, many people believe they are listening but are really planning their next words. Next time you're in a debate, pay attention to whether you do anything like that.

Communication that works is two-way. Try to pay attention to what your spouse is saying, even if it's challenging. Please refrain from interfering. Don't put up a fight. At this point, clarify it for your partner that you have listened carefully to his speech by simply repeating what he said. You'll learn more about them, and they'll be more receptive to what you have to say as a result of this activity.

4.7.3 See Things from Their Point of View

Most of us want to be heard and understood when we're in a fight. We try to persuade the other person to see things from our perspective by talking a lot. This is reasonable, but putting too much emphasis on our need to be understood might backfire. Ironically, when we constantly do this, there isn't much attention paid to the other person's perspective, and neither one feels heard.

If you can see the other person's perspective, you will be able to express yourself better. If others believe they have been heard, they are more inclined to pay attention.

4.7.4 Empathy Is the Best Response to Criticism

In the face of criticism, it is tempting to believe that the person criticizing you is incorrect and get defensive. There is value in hearing the anguish of the other person and responding to their sentiments with empathy, even though criticism is difficult to hear and frequently exaggerated. Look for the truth in what they say as well; this might provide you with useful information.

4.7.5 Acquire What Is Yours

Self-awareness is a virtue, not a weakness. Admitting when you're incorrect is an important part of effective communication. If you and your partner are jointly to blame for a disagreement, identify and accept your share of the blame. It calms things down, sets a good example, and positively demonstrates maturity. It's also common for the other person to reply in kind, bringing you both closer to a solution and mutual understanding.

32

4.7.6 Messages that Begin with "I" Are More Effective

If you're going to criticize someone, start your sentences with "I". Express your frustration by saying something like, "I'm angry when this occurs". If the other person doesn't feel as if they are being attacked, they will be more open to hearing your side of the story.

4.7.7 Compromise May Be Found

Unlike just attempting to "win" a debate, strive to find solutions that satisfy everyone's wants and requirements, whether via compromise or a new, innovative approach that offers you both what you desire most. Focusing on the common good is much more successful than trying to obtain one's own way at the cost of another. Finding a solution that both parties can be pleased with is an important part of good communication.

4.7.8 Take a Breather

When people's emotions are high, it's tough to keep a conversation from devolving into a conflict. Take a break if you or your spouse are becoming too enraged to be productive, or if you see any toxic communication patterns emerging.

That doesn't mean you shouldn't take a stroll and come back to the talk after half an hour, but it does imply you should "sleep on it" so that your feelings can be processed more fully.

4.7.9 Don't Give Up!

If you need to go away from the conversation for a moment, do so. Both of you can work on the conflict's resolution with a positive attitude, mutual respect, and a desire to see the other's standpoint or at the very least come up with an alternative solution. Do not give up on communicating until it is time to end the relationship.

4.7.10 Ask for Advice

Seeing a therapist may help if you or your spouse have problems being polite in the midst of an argument, or if you've attempted to resolve the dispute with your partner on your own, but the situation hasn't improved.

Counseling for couples or families may assist in resolving arguments and teach methods for avoiding future arguments. Even if your spouse does not like to accompany you, traveling alone may frequently be advantageous in many ways as well as saving you money. As a way to strengthen your relationship, it's also possible to utilize applications like Happy Couple.

4.8 The Power of Non-Verbal Communication in Relationships

Effective communication is the lifeblood of relationships, and it extends beyond the realm of spoken or written words. Among the most vital, yet often overlooked, aspects of communication are non-verbal cues. Our body language, facial expressions, gestures, and even silence, communicate volumes about our feelings and intentions.

4.8.1 Reading Beyond Words

Every nod, smile, crossed arms, and widened eyes speak subtly, but directly to our partners. A warm smile can express affection, while crossed arms may indicate discomfort or defensiveness. In a relationship, these unspoken languages create a web of mutual understanding, typically more powerful and profound than verbal exchange.

4.8.2 The Honesty of Non-Verbal Communication

Non-verbal cues are honest; they offer a window into our genuine emotions, sometimes revealing feelings we might not yet be ready to articulate. By paying attention to these cues, couples can deepen their understanding of each other and address issues before they escalate.

Mastering non-verbal communication involves both expressing oneself effectively and interpreting the partner's cues accurately. It's about cultivating an emotional awareness that translates subtle body signals into meaningful information.

4.8.3 The Significance of Touch

In a romantic partnership, touch is a potent form of non-verbal communication. It fosters connection, expresses desire, provides comfort, and can even resolve conflict. From holding hands to a nice caress, these forms of touch can communicate love and belongingness more powerfully than words.

4.8.4 The Art of Listening

Active listening is an integral part of non-verbal communication. It involves being fully present, making eye contact, showing empathy, and providing non-verbal feedback, which reassures your partner that they're heard and valued.

Remember, non-verbal communication plays a significant role in building a strong connection and deeper intimacy. By consciously practicing it, couples can foster a more fulfilling and harmonious relationship.

4.9 Steps to Resolving Differences

It takes time and effort to become proficient at conflict resolution. Remember that each disagreement is unique and has a variety of components. You will fail in every fight if you use the same tactics every time. When it comes to resolving differences, there are certain predictable patterns and helpful tactics that you may use.

- Analyze the cause of the dispute and try to find a solution. Are you aware of what's going on? Why do you believe this? Take some time to ponder the issue at hand and your perceptions of the struggle.

- Initiate the action. Discuss the disagreement at a private location away from the presence of youngsters. Focusing on listening and speaking is easier when there are fewer interruptions.

- Open-ended inquiries are the best way to get to the heart of the matter. A desire to comprehend the other person's standpoint is shown by these inquiries, which may be difficult to answer. Listen to all aspects of a conversation, even if you don't fully agree. Giving voice to your disagreement and expressing your thoughts could put you in danger of not being able to find a solution!

- Constantly communicate with one other. Every party involved deserves a chance to be heard. Make it a priority to communicate genuinely and honestly. People should be allowed to take breaks when they need to. Some people find it difficult to talk about conflict, and others find it simple. You must ensure that everyone has a fair shot at participating in the process.

- Be controlling your strong emotions. Both of you may experience sentiments of irritation, rage, and grief as a result of the conversation you've just had. Take a break and agree to re-engage later, or just stop to give yourself time to reflect. Conflict is difficult and may often surprise us in how it affects us emotionally.

- Take a long-term view of things. Yes, it's crucial to know how we ended ourselves in this situation. Focus on what you both want and need and the best ways to get there.

- Set a deadline for putting the agreed-upon solution into action. There are instances when disagreement can't be settled with a "simple" solution.

You and the other person should agree on the measures to be done, who is accountable for them, and when they should be completed. There should be a follow-up communication to check that the solution has worked, and the problem has been settled. One of these steps/measures that hold the most weightage is using 'Open-ended Questions' as a means to terminate your personal conflict.

4.10 Open-ended Questions—Preferable Inquiring Strategy

An effective dispute resolution strategy is to ask the proper questions. Interpersonal issues may be resolved through the use of a wide variety of questions. Closed-end, clarifying, and open-ended questions are the three main categories of survey questions. Participants in conflict resolution training are taught how to ask effective questions. Learn how to organize questions, which sort of question to use when, and the impact of certain questions. When it comes to asking inquiries, timing is everything.

Start with open-ended inquiries rather than ones aimed at finding the "heart" of the issue as you see it. Too much attention to the minutiae might lead you to overlook the crux of their issue.

4.10.1 Definition

Open-ended questions are the most effective in resolving disputes. There is no one-word response to a question like this. Openness and sharing of ideas are encouraged. Here are a few general-purpose questions that may be utilized on almost any occasion if you don't like open-ended ones. Remember, your tone and body language should convey genuine interest, and carefully observe the information revealed in their response.

4.10.2 Examples

The following genre/style of questions are considered to be put under the category of open-ended questions. Both of the partners must prefer using these types of questions instead of closed-ended or probing ones.

- Please let me know what happened?

- If you could choose your way, what would you prefer to happen?

- How would you describe it?

- The question is, what would it take for us to progress?

- Are there any suggestions you have that would fulfill the demands of both of us at the same time?

- How did you feel about that?

- Is there anything that might really go wrong if you don't make any progress?

- What are you worried about?

- Then, why is it so essential to you?

4.10.3 Acquisitive Questions

Let's imagine you've reached the following conclusion or judgment: You did this purposely to harm me! What if I respond to this claim with a simple question: Did you do this intentionally to harm me? As long as the tone of voice is calm, the query appears to be a real inquiry, even if the conclusion is part of it. Rather than stifling conversation, this kind of inquiry, might open things up. Asking an open-ended question instead of a closed-ended one may provide better results. Did you consider the implications for me?

4.10.4 The 'Why' Type Questions

Asking 'Why' as the first question in an open-ended inquiry may seem to be an excellent technique to boost comprehension. This has been called into doubt in light of certain recent findings. Why questions might be misconstrued as an aggressive challenge, especially in tense situations, it's best to avoid using the word "Why" when you're attempting to be sensitive and avoid causing additional disagreement.

4.11 Enhance Your Innovative Problem-Solving Skills in Couple Communication

Let's consider a real-life couple scenario to better understand this section.

Problem: One partner consistently feels unheard and unappreciated because their partner seems unresponsive during conversations about shared responsibilities. This is causing emotional distress and discontent in the relationship.

Before jumping to conclusions, we must ask: How often does this happen? What are the specific instances? Are there any additional factors at play?

Upon deeper examination, it becomes clear that this issue arises primarily in the evenings, when the unresponsive partner returns from work. The unresponsive partner also confirms feeling exhausted after work, making it difficult to engage in meaningful discussions.

Possible solutions could include scheduling important discussions for a more convenient time, implementing a 'decompression' period post-work, or using more direct communication methods.

However, to prevent miscommunication or any feelings of neglect, the couple agrees on a compromise: They will schedule significant discussions for weekend mornings, when both partners are less likely to be tired or distracted. Furthermore, they decide to check in with each other daily about their emotional and physical states to foster mutual understanding and respect.

After a week, they plan to reassess this arrangement for effectiveness and make necessary adjustments.

This example shows that a problem initially attributed to one partner was more complex. Rather than placing blame, they asked probing questions and communicated effectively to identify the root cause and resolve their issue.

Chapter 5: Embracing Empathy for Enhanced Communication with Your Partner

Building an intimate connection with your partner is essential to having a fulfilling and lasting relationship. Becoming vulnerable within your relationship and discovering methods to be more empathic may help enhance the emotional link between you and your spouse, even during the honeymoon period.

Understanding another person's standpoint implies that you can empathize with them. To establish a long-term love relationship, it is essential to be empathic in all your relationships. Regardless of how long you've had a relationship with your significant other, it's important to feel understood and heard. However, to fully comprehend what it implies to be empathic, it is necessary to distinguish this quality from sympathy. "There are times when empathy is more powerful than compassion. There are several ways to express empathy, but one of the most common is saying, "I'm so pleased you told me that." Barbara Cunningham, a registered marital and family therapist, spoke with *Bustle* about her work.

If you employ emotional, cognitive, or humanitarian empathy, your connection may improve and become stronger. This is where I'm stumped. Empathy is an essential skill to have during dating and in relationships.

5.1 Put Yourself in Their Shoes

You and your partner's relationship may be strengthened if you show empathy. As a result, placing yourself in their shoes is one of the most effective strategies for developing empathy. "If you don't have empathy, you may not know how you feel in different circumstances. An excellent place to begin is to remind individuals that life is a kaleidoscope of happy, unpleasant, and neutral events. A person's ability to comprehend other people's perspectives on life will be enhanced due to this practice, which creates brain connections that develop over time." Laurel Steinberg, Ph.D., a

therapist, relationship specialist in New York City, and an adjunct psychology profes-
sor at Columbia University, told *Bustle* via email.

5.2 Communicate Regarding Their Emotions

According to Steinberg, speak to your spouse in a way that shows you care about
what they're going through. It's important to show your spouse that you comprehend
what they are going through, rather than simply rejecting their feelings by listening
to what they have to say.

5.3 Be Active by Asking Questions

Knowing your partner's emotional state might help you recognize their moods without mentioning them. This is a sign that you care about their happiness and engage
in the connection. Rather than waiting to be informed, they might ask their partners
how things have been going in advance, adds Steinberg.

5.4 Learn to Withhold Judgement

Growing and developing together is an essential component of a successful relationship. Helping one another in times of need involves not making others feel inferior or
judging them. "They don't have to pass judgement on their partner's decisions and
may assume that those decisions were made after considerable deliberation, regardless of whether they were successful. Good things happen when people believe that
their spouses are caring and clever," says Steinberg.

5.5 Take Some of Your Partner's Responsibilities

Taking on some of your partner's errands and everyday obligations might help you
be more empathic in long-term partnerships. This allows you to step into your partner's shoes, helps you judge him less, and at the same time relieves him of his
workload; rest assured that these efforts of yours will not go unnoticed according to
your partner. According to Steinberg, this is one of the best ways to show empathy in
long-term relationships. "A great approach to express empathy in a long-term relationship," adds Steinberg.

5.6 Consider the Partner's Wants and Needs

According to Steinberg, empathizing with a partner's viewpoint "helps to maximize decision-making since it allows for genuine evaluation of a partner's needs and wishes before acting." Preventing resentment between you and your spouse may make you both happy, whether you purchase milk before they inquire or give them treats when they're feeling depressed.

5.7 Learn How to Become More Empathetic Over Your Time

Even if you aren't in school, it's a great idea to broaden your horizons, particularly if it would improve your romantic connection. When it comes to being empathic toward one another, "some couples struggle since having empathy is just a high-order relationship ability," says Steinberg.

5.8 Be Present Once Your Partner Requires You

"Understanding the importance of empathizing with one's spouse might help couples emphasize this ability in a relationship. No matter how difficult a situation may be for one of the partners, they must remain attentive to their partner's emotions, even though their own may be clouding their judgment. Because one partner's hardships typically substantially impact the other, this will be a constant two-way street." According to Steinberg, this is true. Even though it might be difficult to see your spouse go through difficult moments, it is crucial to be around them even in the most difficult situations. Instead of advising them to get through it, put yourself in their shoes.

5.9 Strive for Compassion

Being empathetic all the time might lead to mental exhaustion, since your partner's feelings may become your own. You may assist ease this by showing greater compassion in your relationship. To express compassion, you must feel warm and concerned about your partner's well-being without overloading yourself with absorbing their feelings. This is a wonderful strategy if you'd like to, at the same time, show empathy without sacrificing your sense of self.

Chapter 6: Creating a Higher Sense of Intimacy with Your Partner

Intimacy holds the key to enduring relationships. Physical and emotional closeness are essential components of a healthy relationship. A deficit in closeness can make sustaining a relationship challenging, possibly leading to feelings of loneliness and resentment due to the lack of connection. Your entire well-being grows thanks to the level of intimacy you establish with your lover. Read on for 10 ideas to boost the intimacy level in your relationship if you're concerned about the amount of intimacy within a relationship.

6.1 Try Something New

Having a set schedule each day might give you a sense of security and comfort. This gives you the comfortable feeling of predicting what might happen in the future and, as a result, it might give you some sense of security in your relationship. However, if you want to keep your relationship fresh and exciting, you may want to try something new and unexpected. Trying new experiences, in every aspect of your relationship, takes you out of your comfort zone and this can make you grow individually and as a couple, making your bond stronger. Regardless of what you're doing, it doesn't matter. To spice things up a little, do something new in the bedroom, or learn something new as a couple. As a result of your shared enthusiasm about doing something new, you may become more receptive to one another's company.

6.2 Reminisce

Take a moment to reminisce on the happy experiences you've had together. Having fun together, or seeing something amusing, might bring you back to those times and bring back memories of the encounter. Some good sentiments associated with enjoyable events might be re-experienced when one thinks back on memories. Focus on the happy times and how things were then if you want to improve the closeness in your relationship. Recalling the good times in your partnership may increase your relationship connection by focusing on the positive aspects of your relationship.

6.3 Touch More

This keeps you and your spouse close by maintaining physical touch. Touch is fundamental to healthy development right from childhood, and it carries multiple health benefits. Physical contact, through skin sensors, activates specific nerve fibers; the brain, at this point, stimulates the release of oxytocin, also known as the love hormone, which also has beneficial effects on health. This applies to the person who receives the touch and also to the person who gives it. From today, therefore, you cannot help but touch and hug even more the person you love. When you're out for a stroll, hold hands, sit next to them, and hug them; take your time. To build closeness, spend more time caressing one another.

6.4 Schedule Sex

Get your sex back on the list of things to do. Even though it doesn't appear romantic, life might come in the way of a sexual relationship if it isn't planned in time. Sleep might be the only thing to consider when you finally go to bed when you've had a hard day. When you're not used to having sex, it's simpler to give it up. However, if sexual intimacy is part of your daily routine, it will continue to be an essential aspect of your partnership. It is possible to develop anticipation and activate the largest erogenous zone, the brain, with scheduled sex. Before the sex date, you might exchange text messages outlining what you'd want to do and how seductive your partner is. It also allows you to get ready for some quality alone time with each other. Unexpected sexual encounters are more likely when you have a regularly scheduled time of intimate relations with your partner.

6.5 Stay Connected

Stay connected with your partner all day long. Let your spouse know about how your day is progressing by texting or writing them a message. Once a day, take the person you love and look each other in the eye for at least four to five minutes. Turn off the television and smartphone and dedicate these minutes of silence, intensity, and pure connection to yourselves.

Try to learn about your partner's daily routine and share your own. Spend the nights together. Talk about stuff apart from the kids, housework, and routines. Your degree of closeness will rise if you and your companion have a deep connection.

6.6 Show Appreciation

The simple act of saying please and thank you may go a long way toward making your spouse feel valued. Having a sense of appreciation from your spouse helps you perform the duties that keep your home running smoothly. Be detailed and honest while praising someone. Compliment your mate as much as you can. Tell them what you adore about them. You and your partner will benefit from little words of appreciation and acts of kindness. Your relationship will be much more fulfilling and stable if you know your spouse takes care of you.

6.7 Go to a Date

Take your partner out of the house for a different and romantic evening. Set aside some time to spend with your spouse in a setting where the attention is solely on you. When you're at home, it's easy to be sidetracked by your children, job, or household tasks. It will be a moment just for the two of you, in which you will relax and have fun without having the constant daily distractions around. Carve out more time for the two of you, starting to go out more often, even simply for a walk in the places where you met or where you went out together the first times.

6.8 Be Vulnerable

To be welcomed and understood by your spouse, you must be open and vulnerable with them. Being genuine and open might seem daunting at first, but it is essential. Be open and honest with your spouse about how you feel, what bothers you, what makes you excited, what worries you, and what aspirations you have. Don't be afraid to share the things you'd rather not discuss. When you're wounded or uneasy about your relationship, tell your spouse about it. When you think you could be sensitive with your spouse, your connection with them will grow.

6.9 Have a Life Outside Your Relationships

You'll be a better partner if you put yourself first and respect your spouse's particular needs, even if your relationship is your top priority. When you depend solely on your spouse to satisfy your wants, you're setting yourself up for failure in a relationship.

When you're content and fulfilled in various aspects of your life, you can contribute more to your relationship. Set aside some time a week for friends and people you care about and participate in activities you enjoy. Sharing your excitement and nourishment with your spouse outside the relationship is a great way to get closer.

6.10 Support Your Partner

Stay at their side when they require you. Don't hesitate to tell them whether you can or can't assist. Do your best to let your partner know that they can always count on you in case of need. Be a good listener, as it is a rare quality to find and highly valued at the same time. To make the other person feel heard, use fundamental communication skills and repeat what you listen to them say. Put your phone away and avoid any other sources of distraction, so you can offer your whole focus to your spouse. Encourage your spouse and be a dependable ally. As a result of your partner's trust in you, your relationship is likely to be more stable.

It is possible to have a strong relationship between two people who prioritize physical and emotional closeness. If none of the suggestions above work, or if there are additional difficulties in your relationship preventing intimacy, couples therapy may be able to assist. Improving the relationship closeness is worth it since it may strengthen your connection and your entire well-being.

Chapter 7: 26 Essential Exercises to Hone Couple Communication

7.1 Practice 1: Harness Positive Communication to Enhance Your Relationship

Understanding and managing interpersonal dynamics can be challenging, given their complexity. It's especially true in romantic relationships, where expectations and stakes are high. So, how can we navigate this labyrinth to foster a more harmonious bond?

A proactive approach could be to surround ourselves with couples whose relationships we admire and spend time with them, adopting their effective communication habits.

Starting with a solid understanding of the role of positive communication in relationships is wise. Let's consider seven critical ways that open, positive communication can fortify your relationship:

Encourages Respect
Effective communication can foster mutual respect. It signals to your partner that their opinion matters and that you're brave enough to voice your thoughts.

Removes Uncertainty
As the saying goes, truthfulness simplifies life. In relationships, honesty eliminates the stress of remembering lies and fosters transparency, contributing to collective happiness.

Prevents Misunderstandings
Clear communication is crucial to avoid misunderstandings. It's about expressing your feelings and thoughts in a way your partner can comprehend, and expecting the same in return.

Fosters Trust

Trust is an integral part of any relationship. The consistent and honest exchange of thoughts and feelings can cultivate a sense of security, enhancing the relationship's resilience.

Facilitates Mutual Support

Sharing your struggles with your partner allows them to provide emotional and practical support, fostering a sense of teamwork and shared victory when overcoming challenges.

Enhances Love

Just like a flower that needs regular watering, love thrives on continuous, open, and heartfelt communication. It maintains the vibrancy of your connection and the emotional intimacy between you.

Boosts Mood

Sharing your happiness can amplify it, offering your partner a chance to join in your joy. Expressing your positive emotions freely contributes to a happier, healthier relationship.

Positive communication acts as the lifeblood of a relationship, affecting your emotional state, mutual love, and daily stress level. Do you and your partner communicate openly? Reflect on these points to enrich your relationship journey.

....
....
....
....
....
....
....
....

7.1.1 Reflective Questions

1. What forms of communication do you find most effective in your relationship? Are these verbal, non-verbal, or written forms?

2. Are there topics you find difficult to discuss openly with your partner? Why? How can you approach these topics more comfortably?

3. Can you recall a time when clear, honest communication resolved a potential misunderstanding between you and your partner?

4. What is your partner's reaction when you are honest? Does it foster trust and deepen your connection?

5. How do you usually share your struggles or concerns with your partner? Is there room for improvement in this aspect?

6. What can you do to ensure your love is consistently communicated and acknowledged?

7. How often do you share your joys and successes with your partner? How does it influence your overall mood and relationship quality?

8. Reflect on a recent instance where positive communication significantly benefited your relationship. How can you replicate such positive experiences?

9. How would expanding your communication skills affect your relationship in the long term?

10. What is one step you can take today to enhance positive communication in your relationship?

Reflect on these questions, jot down your thoughts, and discuss them with your partner. You may discover new insights about your communication patterns and find ways to enhance them for a more harmonious relationship.

....
....
....
....
....
....
....
....

....
....
....
....
....
....
....
....
....
....
....
....
....
....
....
....
....

7.2 Practice 2: Assertive Communication with Your Partner

In relationships, both partners should be able to express themselves openly, antici-
pate mutual respect, and decline requests without being perceived as unkind. However, in some cases, the inability to say "no" creates a power imbalance, typically when
one partner dominates the conversation or imposes decisions.

The goal is not to address relationships with abuse, but to correct unhealthy communication patterns that might stem from various factors. If there's any form of violence,
seek professional counseling.

Equality can't be measured objectively in relationships. However, both partners
should be able to voice their opinions, make fair demands, and refuse unreasonable
ones. Assertive individuals are open, clear, and collaborative.

Unhealthy communication patterns could be non-assertive, aggressive, or selfish.
Non-assertive people are generally submissive, over-accommodating, and fear con-

frontations. Aggressive individuals tend to dominate conversations and harm their relationships, while selfish individuals focus primarily on their needs and desires.

The communication style of a relationship tends to settle into a pattern over time. Harmony is possible if both parties are polite and assertive, but conflict arises when one or both partners adopt aggressive or passive styles.

7.2.1 Factors Influencing Your Relationship Style

Your relationship style is largely shaped by modeling influences, self-esteem, and self-talk. Modeling influences refer to behaviors and communication styles you observed during childhood, which may be replicated or rejected in your adult relationships.

Self-esteem directly influences how you interact with others, with low self-esteem often leading to passivity and high self-esteem occasionally resulting in egotistical behavior.

Your self-talk, or how you speak to and about yourself, directly impacts how you relate to others. It can perpetuate submissive or aggressive behavior patterns in your relationship.

7.2.2 Strategies for Assertive Communication

Effective strategies include reflective listening, thinking before speaking, using assertive I-Language, and collaborative support. Reflective listening involves understanding the spoken words and nonverbal cues of your partner.

Before speaking, consider whether assertiveness is required and compose your thoughts. I-Language allows you to express your needs without violating your partner's rights or feelings.

Collaborative support involves mutual assistance in adopting assertiveness. As change can be challenging, having a partner to lean on can make it more manageable.

Remember, transitioning to assertive communication may be difficult initially, but it can create a foundation of mutual respect and care, enhancing the overall health of your relationship.

7.2.3 Reflective Exercises and Questions for Developing Assertiveness

To wrap up this section, let's engage in some practical exercises and pose reflective questions that can help you develop and improve assertiveness in your relationship.

Exercise 1: Practice Assertive I-Language

Take turns with your partner discussing different scenarios where you might typically avoid assertiveness. Practice using assertive "I" language to express your feelings and needs in these situations. Remember to respect your partner's feelings and not dismiss their views.

Exercise 2: Role-Playing

Choose different scenarios where assertiveness is required. Role-play these scenarios, taking turns playing both the assertive and non-assertive roles. This allows you to practice your assertiveness skills in a safe environment and provide insights into the perspectives of each other.

Exercise 3: Assertiveness Journal

Start an assertiveness journal. Write about situations where you were successful in being assertive and where you struggled. Reflect on these experiences and discuss them with your partner. This will help you identify patterns and areas for improvement.

Reflective Questions:

1. Reflect on a recent situation where you wished you had been more assertive. How could you have managed it diversely, employing assertive "I" statements?

2. How do your self-esteem and self-talk impact your ability to be assertive in your relationship? What can you do starting today to improve self-esteem and the quality of your self-talk to increase your assertiveness?

3. Identify and discuss a situation where your modeling influences (parents, teachers, etc.) might have shaped your assertiveness or lack thereof.

4. How did you feel during the role-playing exercise? Were you comfortable being assertive? Why or why not?

5. What strategies can you develop to support each other in becoming more assertive?

Remember, becoming more assertive is a journey, not a destination. It takes time and practice, so be patient with yourself and your partner as you navigate this together. Take note of progress and celebrate small victories to keep you motivated and on track.

....
....
....
....
....
....
....
....
....
....
....
....
....
....
....
....
....
....
....
....
....
....
....
....

7.3 Practice 3: Mastering Conflict Resolution in Relationships

Differences of opinion are a normal fact in a relationship. The real challenge lies in managing these disagreements effectively and healthily. Here's a streamlined approach to resolving disputes with your partner:

53

7.3.1 Embrace Open Communication

Transparent discussion about both positives and negatives is key in a sustainable, happy partnership. Sharing openly about issues like finances, goals, and personal challenges without fear of retaliation ensures a balanced, healthy relationship. If fear or frustration obstructs open communication, it could be a sign of an unhealthy dynamic.

7.3.2 Respect in Heat of Argument

Maintain respect, even in heated debates. Keep the focus on the topic, avoiding personal slights or insults. Regular verbal or physical aggression are alarming signs of potential abuse. It's important to ensure discussions are safe, respectful, and non-threatening.

7.3.3 Uncover Unmet Needs

Sometimes, conflicts are expressions of unmet needs. Instead of sweating the small stuff, delve deeper to uncover any larger issues. Try seeing the situation from your partner's perspective: What need are they trying to communicate?

7.3.4 Avoid Control-Based Conflicts

Signs of attempted control in your partner's actions are red flags. Whether it's disapproving of your interactions with others, demanding you change your priorities, or limiting your social activities, no one should exert control over you. Even if justified as "overprotection" or "trust issues", this is unhealthy and could be indicative of abuse.

7.3.5 Seek Compromise

Balance and compromise are crucial. Aim to reach a consensus where both parties' needs are accommodated without excessive compromise. This might involve sharing time between friend groups, or collaborating on household tasks like grocery shopping.

7.3.6 Learn to Let Go

Recognize when it's better to agree to disagree. Is the contention really about the upcoming television program, or the choice of tonight's meal? If it doesn't matter in a week, it's likely not worth an argument. However, consistent, major disagreements might warrant reconsidering the compatibility of the relationship.

7.3.7 Evaluate Resolvability

Important issues like future planning, lifestyle choices, or values can lead to serious disagreements. In these cases, consider whether the issue can be resolved without compromising core values. Successful, long-term relationships often require aligned aspirations, values, and worldviews.

Adhering to these principles will empower you to navigate conflicts in a more constructive and beneficial way. After all, a healthy relationship isn't characterized by constant, escalating conflicts, but by constructive discussions and shared growth. Remember: it's not about becoming the couple from The Notebook; it's about building a strong, respectful, and mutually fulfilling connection.

Exercise 1: Open Communication
Reflect on a recent disagreement with your partner. Did you feel like you could openly express your thoughts and feelings? Were there any topics you avoided discussing? If so, why?

Exercise 2: Maintaining Respect
Think about the last heated argument you had. Were there any moments where you lost respect? Did any comments cross the line into personal insult? Reflect on how you can better maintain respect even when emotions are high.

Exercise 3: Uncover Unmet Needs
Recall a recent conflict. Can you identify any unmet needs that might have caused or escalated the conflict? Discuss these needs with your partner and brainstorm ways to fulfill them.

Exercise 4: Avoiding Control-Based Conflicts
Have you ever experienced a sense that your partner was attempting to dictate your actions or choices? If so, what were the circumstances? Discuss these accidents with your partner and express how they made you feel.

Exercise 5: Seeking Compromise
List five recent disagreements and brainstorm potential compromises for each. Aim to find resolutions that acknowledge and cater to the needs and preferences of both parties.

Exercise 6: Learn to Let Go
Think about the minor issues you've recently argued about. Are there any you could have let go? Practice letting go of small disagreements this week and note any changes in your relationship.

Exercise 7: Evaluating Resolvability

Choose an important issue that's caused disagreement in your relationship. Discuss with your partner whether it's resolvable without compromising your core values or aspirations.

Discussion:

Review these exercises with your partner and discuss your findings. What steps will you take together to expand your conflict resolution skills? How can you secure these practices as part of your sustained communication approach?

Remember, these exercises are not a one-time solution, but a continual practice. Aim to revisit them regularly to further elevate your conflict resolution skills and enhance your relationship.

....
....
....
....
....
....
....
....
....
....
....
....
....
....
....
....
....
....

....
....
....
....
....

7.4 Practice 4: Mastering Constructive Discussions

Certain topics can feel like a minefield in any relationship. However, the key is to approach these discussions constructively. The goal isn't about proving who's right, but rather finding a mutually beneficial resolution. Here's how to facilitate such conversations effectively.

7.4.1 Ditch the 'Right or Wrong' Mindset

Realize that discussions aim to solve an issue affecting you both. The focus should be on working together towards a positive shift. Plus, embracing diverse perspectives often sparks creative solutions.

7.4.2 Timing is Everything

Avoid discussions when one of you is stressed or distracted. Opt for a moment when both of you are at ease and receptive. If you sense that the timing isn't right, don't hesitate to reschedule. This way, the conversation benefits you both.

7.4.3 Start Positively

Appreciating your partner's willingness to discuss sensitive issues can set a cooperative tone. You might begin by saying, "I truly value your willingness to talk about this. Your input is invaluable to me."

7.4.4 Keep it Focused

Avoid veering off-topic or bringing up past issues. If the discussion starts to derail, politely steer it back by saying, "Let's focus on one thing at a time."

7.4.5 Practice Active Listening

Successful conversations hinge on good listening. Focus on your partner's words without planning your next response, avoid judging and be open even if they are thoughts that differ from yours.

57

To strengthen this skill, consider engaging in the following exercises:

Exercise 1: Choose a controversial topic, and take turns discussing your views without interrupting each other. Reflect on how it felt to listen without interruption and how it influenced the discussion.

Exercise 2: Develop the Habit of Well-Timed Conversations. Select a moment when both of you are in a relaxed state and receptive to dialogue. Note the difference in your communication compared to conversations held during stress.

Exercise 3: Role-play a conversation, with one person intentionally straying off-topic. The other person practices steering the conversation back to the issue at hand. Reflect on the techniques that worked best.

Remember, practicing these skills regularly will help make them a habit, improving your communication over time.

....
....
....
....
....
....
....
....
....
....
....
....
....
....
....
....
....
....

....
....
....
....
....
....
....

7.5 Practice 5: Fostering a Robust Connection

Fulfilling relationships contribute to health, happiness, and stress reduction. Each relationship is unique, yet some principles universally apply. These insights can enhance not only romantic partnerships but also professional and familial ones.

Acknowledge individuality. You can't meet all expectations, and you shouldn't aim to change others. Recognize the unique individuality of each person.

Practice active listening. Being fully present during conversations fosters understanding. Absorb their story as if you're experiencing it, thereby cultivating deeper comprehension.

Express curiosity. Show interest in their thoughts and emotions. Sharing knowledge can form more profound bonds, but avoid oversharing.

Embrace adaptability. Change is inevitable and can sometimes cause stress, but flexibility is key.

Prioritize self-care. Balanced relationships cater to the needs of both parties.

Cultivate trust. Follow through on your commitments to foster reliance in a relationship.

Manage conflict. Disputes are normal. Breathe before discussing disagreements. Use "I statements" to communicate your feelings and views without laying blame on the other party. Ensure your language is unambiguous, succinct, and refrain from placing blame.

Take responsibility. Apologies, when sincere, can mend fractured relationships.

Know that resolution takes time. Some issues require patience, open communication, and sensitivity. Listen intently, propose suitable solutions, and implement them promptly while allowing for future adjustments.

Stay positive. Balance each negative interaction with multiple positive ones.

Maintain perspective. Engage in fulfilling activities outside the relationship and stay true to yourself.

To enrich this practice, consider the following exercises:

Exercise 1: Role-play a conversation about a disagreement. Practice using "I statements," keeping language clear and concise, and focusing on one issue at a time.

Exercise 2: Reflect on a recent conflict. How might you have managed it differently? How can you take responsibility and apologize sincerely?

Exercise 3: Write a list of activities you enjoy outside your relationship. Plan to engage in one of these activities in the upcoming week. Reflect on how it feels to nurture your needs and interests.

Reflect also on these questions:

1. How have you recently demonstrated active listening in a conversation with your partner? Can you share an instance where being fully present in a conversation made a significant impact?

2. Can you recall a time when adaptability played a crucial role in managing a conflict within your relationship? How did your flexibility contribute to the resolution of the issue?

3. Reflect on your balance of self-care and nurturing the relationship. Are there areas in your life where you could prioritize self-care more, and how might this benefit your relationship?

The regular application of these skills can significantly strengthen your relationship, promote understanding, and ensure constructive conflict resolution.

....
....
....

....

....

....

....

....

....

....

....

....

....

....

....

....

....

....

....

....

....

....

....

....

....

7.6 Practice 6: Cultivating Emotional Intimacy

Emotional intimacy, a cornerstone of love relationships, rivals physical closeness in importance. It is the shared vulnerability and understanding between partners. Emotional intimacy fosters a sense of security in the relationship and promotes a stronger bond. Without it, feelings of anger, insecurity, or loneliness may creep in, compromising the relationship.

7.6.1 Importance of Emotional Intimacy

Emotional intimacy enables you to be authentically yourself, without fear of jeopardizing the relationship. Its absence can diminish feelings of safety, support, love, and overall connectedness, even impacting physical intimacy. As relationship therapist Rachel Wright asserts, a long-term relationship is unlikely without emotional intimacy.

7.6.2 Enhancing Emotional Intimacy

Creating emotional closeness is a journey. Here are some immediate strategies to help nurture it:

7.6.2.1 Show Vulnerability

Sharing hidden truths or feelings, or narrating an unshared experience, helps to create a bond. Psychologist Paul Hokemeyer suggests strategic vulnerability – exposing a single aspect of yourself to start.

7.6.2.2 Affirmations and Compliments

Regularly acknowledging your partner's qualities fosters mutual appreciation. A simple "I love you" or an acknowledgment of their effort can go a long way.

7.6.2.3 Value Sexual Satisfaction

Research suggests sexually satisfied couples experience stronger emotional bonds. Spend time understanding and fulfilling each other's desires.

7.6.2.4 Break the Routine

Try activities that you enjoyed during the courtship period. Shared experiences can bring back feelings of joy and closeness.

Consider these exercises to bolster emotional intimacy:

Exercise 1: Share a personal story or hidden truth with your partner, paving the way for mutual vulnerability.

Exercise 2: Practice giving daily affirmations or compliments to your partner. Reflect on how it changes the energy of the relationship.

Exercise 3: Discuss your desires and work together to improve your sexual satisfaction.

Exercise 4: Plan an activity outside your usual routine. Reflect on how this change invigorates your relationship.

Regular investment in emotional intimacy will strengthen the connection and fortify your relationship against potential challenges.

....

....

....

....

....

....

....

....

....

....

....

....

....

....

....

....

....

....

....

....

....

....

....

7.7 Practice 7: Enhancing Physical Intimacy

Physical intimacy is a crucial aspect of a relationship, encompassing more than just sex. It includes your relationship dynamics, emotional bonds, and chemistry. Despite regular stressors, it's essential to maintain this physical closeness. Though daily sex isn't a requirement for a healthy relationship, maintaining a rhythm and deep connection is vital.

63

7.7.1 Open Discussion

Open conversation about your sexual desires and expectations can alleviate misunderstandings. Often, the desire for physical intimacy varies between partners. If you express your needs openly, you're less likely to feel disconnected. According to sexologist Valeria Chuba, a shared understanding of intimacy's value is crucial. Ensure these conversations are open and nonjudgmental.

7.7.2 Non-sexual Touch

Creating a "culture of touch" can foster closeness outside the bedroom. A simple morning kiss, for example, might set the tone for a more intimate evening. Moreover, understanding your partner's 'love language' can deepen your emotional and physical bond.

7.7.3 Foreplay

Establishing an environment conducive to sex, via cuddling, massage, or romantic readings, can encourage a desire for more intimacy. Remember, each person experiences pleasure differently, so explore together.

7.7.4 Mutual Satisfaction

In a long-term relationship, physical intimacy isn't just about pleasure—it's about maintaining a spark. Over time, sexual desires fluctuate due to age or stress. Dr. Chaves suggests altering routines to keep your sexual experiences fresh.

Here are some exercises to help improve physical intimacy:

Exercise 1: Have a candid conversation about your expectations and desires for physical intimacy.

How do your desires and expectations for physical intimacy align with those of your partner? Are there any discrepancies, and if so, how can you work together to bridge these gaps?

Exercise 2: Establish a "culture of touch" in your relationship. Monitor how this changes your relationship's dynamic.

How do you feel when practicing the "culture of touch" in your relationship? Do you feel closer? More connected? Are there any changes you could make to enhance this practice?

Exercise 3: Engage in regular non-sexual intimacy practices like cuddling or massages. Reflect on how this affects your sexual relationship.

Have you tried varying your sexual routine? How have these variations impacted your mutual satisfaction and physical intimacy in your relationship?

Exercise 4: Experiment with changes in your sexual routine. Discuss how these variations influence your mutual satisfaction.

Are there moments when your desire for sex increases and others when it decreases? How do you manage life's stresses to maintain a healthy libido?

Physical intimacy is a journey, as unique as your relationship. Take time to understand each other's needs and work together to meet them.

....

....

....

....

....

....

....

....

....

....

....

....

....

....

....

....

....

....

7.8 Practice 8: Shared Responsibility in Partnership

Research at Missouri University suggests that marital satisfaction increases when couples share household and child-rearing responsibilities. This doesn't necessarily mean an equal division of tasks, but rather shared tasks agreed upon by both parties. As Adam Galovan, a Ph.D. student, illustrates, "For instance, one might cook dinner while the other takes care of the children. The key is engaging in activities together with an agreed-upon division of work."

Galovan's study of 160 heterosexual couples found that when women perceived their husbands as actively participating in household chores, it strengthened their marital bonds. Furthermore, wives reported happier relationships when their husbands were connected to their children, highlighting the importance of a strong father-child relationship.

Adjusting to parenthood can bring stress to a marriage. To cope, Galovan advises couples to seize daily moments of connection, even in mundane tasks like dishwashing. These small, shared experiences can greatly enhance marital satisfaction.

Here are three exercises to implement this practice:

1. **Responsibility Swap**: For a week, swap some of your responsibilities. It's a great way to appreciate each other's contributions and experience different aspects of your shared life.

2. **Parenting Participation**: If you have children, ensure both partners have special time with them individually. This not only strengthens parental bonds but also gives each partner a chance to rest or engage in personal activities.

3. **Daily Shared Activity**: Find a simple daily task you can do together, like cleaning up after dinner. It's a small but significant way to connect and share responsibilities.

Reflect on these questions together:

1. How do we currently divide responsibilities, and how does it affect our relationship?

2. How can we better balance or share tasks to improve our connection and mutual satisfaction?

3. How can we ensure both partners actively participate in parenting, and what changes might this require in our daily routines?

....
....
....
....
....
....
....
....
....
....
....
....
....
....
....
....
....
....
....
....

7.9 Practice 9: Emotional Management Mastery

Emotions, whether stemming from relationships, work, self-perception, or other life experiences, are an integral part of us. However, these feelings can sometimes lead to emotional exhaustion. When confronted with potent emotions like anger, despair, or even overwhelming joy, it's essential to maintain balance. So, how do you navigate these emotional landscapes?

Here are three exercises to enhance your emotional management skills:

1. **Emotion Journaling**: Keep a daily journal of your emotions. Note what you feel, the intensity, and possible triggers. It's an excellent tool for understanding your emotional patterns and identifying any recurring stressors.

2. **Mindfulness Practice**: Incorporate mindfulness exercises, like meditation, into your routine. These techniques encourage emotional awareness and help you to react more thoughtfully when strong emotions arise.

3. **Emotion Regulation Techniques**: Learn and practice emotion regulation strategies, such as deep breathing or progressive muscle relaxation, which can provide immediate relief from intense emotions.

Reflect on these questions to understand your emotional management:

1. How do I currently react when I experience strong emotions, and how does it impact me and those around me?

2. What patterns do I notice in my emotional responses, and what triggers seem to provoke intense feelings?

3. What techniques or strategies can I employ to better manage my emotions and respond effectively in various situations?

....

....

....

....

....

....

....

....
....
....
....
....
....
....
....
....
....
....
....
....
....
....
....
....

7.10 Practice 10: Fostering Openness and Trust

Trust is a pillar in a relationship, and when it gets shaken, a relationship can crumble. Therefore, developing and maintaining trust is critical. However, cultivating trust can be challenging, given the intricate web of experiences that shape our capacity to rely on others.

7.10.1 Overcoming the Trust Cycle

Trust issues in a relationship can spread like wildfire, starting with simple doubts and escalating to suspicion and distress. To break this cycle, reflect on the roots of your distrust and consider how your fear might be impacting your perception of your partner's actions. Ask yourself:

1. How can I begin to dispel this cycle of distrust?

2. What stories am I telling myself that feed my insecurities?

69

3. Is my distrust a reflection of the present or a residue of experiences?

....
....
....
....
....
....
....
....
....
....
....
....
....
....
....
....
....
....
....
....
....

Trust can be restored by adopting a few approaches:

1. Embrace Vulnerability: Share your feelings, fears, and dreams openly with your partner.

2. Presume Positive Intentions: Even when they disappoint you, remind yourself that they may have simply made a mistake.

3. Promote Open Communication: Address concerns head-on instead of letting them fester.

4. Understand the Influence of Past Pain: Recognize how previous experiences can impact your current trust levels.

5. Listen to Your Intuition: Trust your instincts and communicate any discomforts promptly to avoid misunderstandings.

6. Learn to Reconcile: After disagreements, make efforts to mend bonds and return to peaceful communication.

7. Express Your Needs Clearly: Make your expectations explicit to avoid frustration and disappointment.

7.10.2 Rebuilding Broken Trust

Often, relationships move through cycles of harmony, conflict, and restoration. However, some get stuck in the conflict phase. Before exploring common strategies to rebuild trust, jot down your thoughts on how you could regain your partner's trust. Remember, no one understands your relationship better than you.

Once you've reflected, consider these steps to rebuild broken trust:

1. Schedule a discussion to share thoughts about the breach of trust without blaming or criticizing.

2. Listen to each other non-judgmentally and express your feelings.

3. Acknowledge your roles in the situation and take responsibility.

4. Offer sincere apologies and accept the ones given.

5. Develop a plan to prevent future breaches of trust.

7.11 Practice 11: Mastering the Art of Listening

A Healthy and Efficient communication within a relationship isn't merely about expressing yourself, but it presupposes, above all, attentive listening. Amidst our daily distractions, truly tuning in to our partner's words can be challenging, but it is fundamental to a strong connection. Here, we'll explore five key strategies to enhance your listening skills.

1. **Empathetic Listening**: Step into your partner's shoes. Understanding their experiences and perspective helps to foster a sense of security, allowing more open communication. Try to relate to their situations, such as workplace stress or home concerns, to better grasp their emotional state.

2. **Emotional Listening**: Recognize your partner's feelings. Whether they're expressing anger, sorrow, or joy, your ability to respond effectively hinges on your understanding of their emotional state. This understanding can prevent exacerbating their feelings with an inappropriate response.

3. **Unbiased Listening**: Listen objectively, especially during disagreements. Each partner's views deserve acknowledgment. Filtering your partner's words through your biases hinders true understanding. While you don't have to change your views, do try to comprehend their perspective.

4. **Loving Listening**: Non-verbal cues, like eye contact or a comforting touch, can demonstrate your interest and respect for your partner's words. Show that you're fully present, removing distractions like gadgets, and focus solely on them.

5. **Generous Listening**: Devote time and attention to your partner. An open line of communication requires commitment, allowing your partner to freely express their thoughts and emotions.

Exercises:
1. Practice empathy: Spend a day trying to view situations from your partner's perspective.

2. Active emotional listening: Next time your partner talks about their day, attempt to identify the emotions they're expressing and reflect them back.

3. Unbiased listening challenge: During your next disagreement, try to understand your partner's standpoint without letting your bias interfere.

Reflection Questions:
1. When was the last time you genuinely listened, empathized, and responded to your partner's feelings?

2. Can you recall a situation where your bias might have hindered effective listening?

3. How could you make your listening more loving and generous?

....
....
....
....
....
....
....
....
....
....
....
....
....
....
....
....
....
....
....
....
....
....
....
....

7.12 Practice 12: Developing Emotional Accuracy

Understanding your partner's emotions is a key aspect of a thriving relationship. However, it's not only about identifying emotions but also discerning when certain feelings, such as anger or contempt, can be damaging. Studies suggest that "empathic accuracy" – the ability to accurately read your partner's feelings – can influence how one responds to their partner's requests and ultimately affect relationship quality.

Couples who can accurately recognize appeasement emotions like embarrassment tend to have healthier relationships than those where dominant emotions like anger or contempt prevail. It's vital to comprehend how accurately identifying various types of emotions can impact interpersonal relationships.

While disagreements are inevitable even in strong relationships, it's how we navigate these emotionally charged situations that matters. For example, a request for personal change in a partner may stir up negative feelings. But if you can accurately pick up on your partner's appeasing emotions like embarrassment, it demonstrates that you value their feelings and understand the request can be upsetting.

However, correctly reading "dominance emotions" like anger or contempt in your partner can harm the relationship. It's crucial to find a balance between being sensitive to your partner's feelings and not letting negative emotions dominate the relationship.

7.12.1 The Role of Flexibility

Flexibility in a relationship implies being open to change and dealing with emotionally intense situations. Maintaining an emotionally flexible stance allows for healthier communication, thus enhancing the relationship's quality.

7.12.2 The Importance of Direct Communication

Clear communication is crucial in any relationship. Research involving 111 couples showed that expressing and acknowledging emotions is a critical aspect of healthy relationships. Whether positive or negative, direct communication is more beneficial in the long term.

However, the emotional context in which you present your requests for change is crucial. It's okay to feel sheepish or ashamed while discussing sensitive issues, as long as your partner knows you care for them. This indicates your commitment to the relationship and your consideration for their feelings, contributing positively to the relationship.

Exercises:
1. Role-play a situation where one of you asks for change from the other. Try to accurately recognize and respond to each other's emotions.

2. When your partner expresses feelings of embarrassment or shame, let them know you recognize these emotions and value their feelings.

3. Practice clear and direct communication when discussing sensitive issues.

Reflection Questions:

1. Can you recall a situation where empathic accuracy played a significant role in resolving a disagreement?

2. How can you foster flexibility in your relationship?

3. What is the first step you need to take as early as tomorrow to expand your communication skills?

....

....

....

....

....

....

....

....

....

....

....

....

....

....

....

....

....

....

....

7.13 Practice 13: Bridging Communication Gaps

Clear and consistent communication is the cornerstone of a healthy, fulfilling and lasting relationship. However, poor or incomplete communication can create problems, affecting intimacy, conflict resolution, and the overall growth of the relationship. Consequences can include heightened conflict, feelings of neglect or lack of appreciation, loneliness, lack of intimacy, and difficulty in setting and achieving goals.

Signs of poor communication in a relationship can include mocking or insulting each other, dominance, silent treatment, unresolved arguments, lack of compromise, reduced communication efforts, and focusing on the facts of a conflict rather than considering the emotions involved.

7.13.1 Steps to Enhance Relationship Communication
Here are three key approaches that can help:

7.13.1.1 Understand Each Other's Attachment Styles
Every individual has an 'attachment style,' influenced by the care they received from their caregivers during their early years. If one or both partners have an insecure attachment style, it can result in fear-driven rather than sincere communication. Avoidant partners often desire space, so one can respect this need by communicating in small doses and giving them time to process. For anxious partners, reassurance through consistent and proactive communication is essential.

Exercise: Discuss each other's attachment styles and brainstorm ways to accommodate these styles in your communication.

7.13.1.2 Address Meta-Emotional Mismatches
A meta-emotional mismatch occurs when partners have conflicting beliefs about emotions. If one partner believes it's beneficial to discuss and experience emotions and the other thinks it's counterproductive, it can hinder effective communication. Understanding and respecting each other's beliefs about emotions can significantly improve communication.

Exercise: Share your beliefs about emotions based on your experiences and discuss how they affect your communication styles.

7.13.1.3 Resolve Past Issues

Unresolved past issues can impede effective communication. Whether it's a breach of trust or an unaddressed miscommunication, such issues can prevent you from moving forward. It's important to address these issues, rebuild trust, and forgive each other to improve communication.

Exercise: Identify any unresolved issues in your relationship and discuss how you can move past them.

Reflection Questions:

1. How does your attachment style influence your communication in your relationship?

2. Do you think there's a meta-emotional mismatch in your relationship? If so, how can you address it?

3. Are there unresolved issues that might be impacting your communication? How might you collaboratively approach their resolution?

4. What concrete steps can you take to improve communication in your relationship?

....
....
....
....
....
....
....
....
....
....
....

....

....

....

....

....

....

....

....

....

....

....

....

7.14 Practice 14: Understanding and Addressing Your Partner's Issues

In any relationship, tension and misunderstandings can surface, sometimes due to minor accident. It's essential to navigate these moments effectively, as avoiding conflict can result in unresolved feelings and heightened tension.

7.14.1 Identifying the Problem in a Relationship

Effective communication is key to addressing relationship issues. It involves understanding and accepting the emotions involved, and addressing disagreements as a team. It's important to express your concerns freely and constructively.

Consider Bob and Amy's example. Amy preferred to keep only necessary items in their home to minimize clutter, while Bob found importance in various items, including project supplies. Their different perspectives led to a significant argument, and both now have reservations in discussing the issue of clutter.

Identifying the underlying feelings and concerns is crucial in this situation. What is the root of your frustration, and how does it impact your connection as a couple?

7.14.2 Recognizing the Pain

In therapy, Amy expressed that she felt Bob valued his possessions more than her well-being, making her feel unloved. Bob, on the other hand, feared that Amy would always find fault in him. These underlying issues needed to be addressed first before tackling the clutter problem. They found ways to ensure both their needs were met and learned to empathize with each other's pain.

7.14.3 Responding to Relationship Stress

Unresolved issues can impact a person's sense of security in a relationship. It's important to understand and address your partner's distress to maintain connection and trust. The ability to express your concerns and reassure each other of your importance is crucial.

7.14.4 Three Ways to Express Concerns to Your Partner

When addressing relationship concerns, it's important to avoid destructive methods and use constructive approaches instead:

7.14.4.1 Don't Glare

Refrain from pouting, grumbling, or silent treatments. Instead, express your feelings calmly and without blame.

Exercise: "I didn't like the way you spoke to me when you got home."

7.14.4.2 Don't Assume

Don't expect your partner to automatically know your feelings and needs. Communicate clearly about what's bothering you.

Exercise: "I wanted you to understand that I'm feeling stressed from work. Could I vent a bit?"

7.14.4.3 Don't Get Personal

Avoid name-calling or personal insults. Focus on expressing your feelings and experiences without attacking the other person's character.

Exercise: "I get frustrated when there's not enough milk for the kids. I know you didn't mean to forget. What can we do to keep better track of this?"

Reflection Questions:
1. What underlying issues or feelings may be impacting your relationship?

2. How can you express your feelings and requires more effectively to your partner?

3. How can you address the root cause of your frustrations without resorting to personal attacks or silent treatments?

4. What steps can you take to ensure both your needs are met in the relationship?

....
....
....
....
....
....
....
....
....
....
....
....
....
....
....
....
....
....
....
....
....

7.15 Practice 15: Acknowledging Your Partner's Feelings

Good communication is the lifeblood of a healthy relationship, where both individuals feel seen, understood, and secure. When one's feelings or requests for help are met with misunderstanding or defensiveness, it can engender feelings of isolation and insecurity. Here are three listening techniques that can help reconnect with your partner and ensure they feel heard and understood.

Imago Relationship Therapy provides various tools, including a structured conversation method, to help couples enhance their listening skills and foster connection. These include mirroring, validating, and empathizing with your partner.

1. **Mirroring**: This involves reflecting what your partner says to ensure you've accurately understood their perspective. It can be challenging at first, but it gets easier with practice. Start your responses with phrases like "So, I hear you saying…" or "It sounds like you're saying…" This technique can help diffuse defensiveness and foster understanding.

2. **Validating**: This means acknowledging that your partner's feelings and perspective make sense, even if you don't necessarily agree with them. It's about recognizing the validity of their experience. If you're struggling to understand, instead of dismissing their feelings, ask for further clarification with phrases like, "Can you tell me more about…"

3. **Empathizing**: This goes beyond understanding your partner's perspective; it's about connecting with their emotional experience. Phrases like, "It sounds like you were really hurt when…" or "I can imagine how upset you must have felt…" can make a significant difference, showing your partner that you care about their feelings and well-being.

Practicing these skills can create a space where both partners feel heard, understood, and valued, thereby strengthening the relationship. It's important to remember that these techniques require practice, patience, and a commitment to being present and receptive, especially during difficult conversations.

Reflection Questions:
1. How can mirroring, validating, and empathizing enhance communication in your relationship?

2. Can you recall a recent conversation where using one of these techniques could have improved the outcome?

3. What steps can you take to practice these techniques in your daily interactions with your partner?

4. How can these techniques help in diffusing conflict or misunderstanding in your relationship?

7.16 Practice 16: Sharing Your Feelings Openly

Communicating feelings can be challenging, particularly for those less familiar with heart-to-heart exchanges. The vulnerability required to share deeply felt emotions can be daunting. However, this openness cultivates closeness and connection in a relationship.

Here are four guidelines to help you express your feelings effectively:

1. **Accept Your Feelings**: Drop the notion of emotions being good or bad; instead, understand that it's our reactions to these emotions that matter. For instance, being angry does not give a free pass for aggressive behavior. Embrace your negative emotions, but don't let them dictate your actions.

2. **Articulate Your Feelings**: Expressing your feelings, either verbally or in writing, enhances your partner's understanding and empathy. Emotions can often be expressed in simple terms such as angry, attacked, happy, hurt, embarrassed, sad, or scared.

3. **Differentiate Thoughts, Feelings, and Moods**: Feelings are temporary emotional states, while moods last longer. Thoughts reflect your mental processes and perceptions of the world. A helpful guideline is using "I feel" for emotions and "I think" for thoughts. For example, instead of saying, "I think I'm hurt," say, "I feel hurt".

4. **Avoid Judgment**: Refrain from judging your own or your partner's emotions. Dismissing or minimizing feelings can hinder emotional sharing. Respect and validate your partner's feelings instead of offering unsolicited advice or clichés.

To encourage open sharing, express your thoughts and feelings directly to your partner. They can't read your mind. Be sure to share both surface and underlying emotions. You might be angry on the surface but feel hurt or embarrassed deep down. Share your feelings daily, even about seemingly mundane events, to maintain an emotional connection.

Here are three exercises to foster emotional sharing:

1. **Emotional Check-in**: Dedicate a few minutes each day to discuss your emotional state with each other.

2. **Emotion Journaling**: Write about your emotions daily and share entries with each other when comfortable.

3. **Emotion Naming**: Practice identifying and naming your emotions as they arise to build your emotional vocabulary.

Reflect on these questions together:

1. What emotions do you find the most challenging to express, and why?

2. How can you create a safe space for each other to share feelings without judgment?

3. How can daily sharing of emotions strengthen your relationship?

....
....
....
....
....
....
....
....
....
....
....
....
....
....
....
....

....
....
....
....
....
....
....

7.17 Practice 17: The Art of Compromise

Compromise is a crucial relationship skill, applicable in various situations, from travel planning to resolving sexual issues. It's about finding mutually satisfactory solutions, rather than surrendering to one's desires at the cost of the other's comfort. It's not about doing things unwillingly; instead, it centers on mutual understanding and balance. Here are some situations where compromise plays a significant role:

1. **Balancing Time Together vs. Alone**: Compromise ensures that both parties can enjoy their needed levels of alone time and quality couple time. Discuss preferences and make your shared time meaningful.

2. **Managing Family Plans**: During special occasions, families can pull couples in different directions. Establishing traditions or alternating between family visits can help avoid conflict.

3. **Harmonizing Your Sex Life**: Differences in sexual desire can lead to tension. Concentrating on quality rather than quantity can be a reasonable compromise. Consider seeking professional advice if required.

4. **Understanding Love Languages**: Everyone experiences love differently, and compromise can help bridge these differences. Try to understand and "speak" each other's love languages to ensure mutual feelings of security and warmth.

5. **Planning Fair Travels**: Holidays often require adjustments to accommodate each other's desires. Discussing preferences beforehand and creating a balanced wish list can prevent resentment.

6. **Navigating Arguments**: Everyone has their argument style. It's essential to communicate effectively and "fight fair." Compromise in this context means understanding each other's perspectives and finding a shared communication style.

7. **Discussing Finances**: Open conversations about finances can maintain fairness in a relationship. If income levels differ, agree on a fair division of expenses.

Here are three exercises to practice compromise:

1. **Scenario Simulation**: Consider hypothetical situations and discuss how you'd compromise.

2. **Negotiation Practice**: Discuss a current issue and attempt to find a mutually beneficial solution.

3. **Love Language Experiment**: Try to speak each other's love language for a week.

Reflect on these questions:

1. In what areas do you find it hardest to compromise, and why?

2. How can effective compromising strengthen your relationship?

3. Can you identify a recent situation where compromise led to a satisfactory outcome?

....
....
....
....
....
....
....
....
....

....

....

....

....

....

....

....

....

....

....

....

....

....

....

....

7.18 Practice 18: The Power of Partner Mindfulness

Maintaining a healthy relationship requires a balance between personal needs and those of the partnership. It's not about ignoring your needs or focusing solely on your partner, but about mutual respect and consideration for each other's emotions and wishes. This is called "partner mindfulness" – giving nonjudgmental attention and understanding to your partner's desires and needs, both when together and apart.

Many people use mindfulness to manage the needs and wishes of children, friends, and coworkers. However, when it comes to romantic relationships, especially during stress and conflict, they often fail to apply this practice. By practicing partner mindfulness, you can empathize and understand your partner better, which in turn builds connection, reduces conflict, and improves overall satisfaction.

Here are nine easy ways to incorporate partner mindfulness into your routine:

1. Self-awareness: Be honest about your current relationship status. Assess how responsive you are to your partner's desires and needs.

2. Commitment: Make a conscious decision to go the extra mile to enhance your relationship.

3. Focused Attention: Spend some moments focusing solely on your partner – their thoughts, feelings, and needs.

4. Connect Twice Daily: Make sure to greet and farewell each other. These small gestures help refocus on your relationship.

5. Express Gratitude: Regularly express your appreciation towards your partner.

6. Practice Compassion: Show understanding and sympathy when your partner struggles to connect.

7. Response over Reaction: Reconsider your response during a dispute, aiming to reply thoughtfully and compassionately.

8. Active Listening: Pay attention to body language and nonverbal cues during conversations.

9. Maintain Balance: Always consider your partner's desires and needs while making decisions.

Embarking on this shift in your relationship, initially, may seem overwhelming. However, relationships require continuous effort to be rewarding and fulfilling. Moreover, this mindfulness practice sets a great example for children, teaching them about healthy relationships.

Try implementing these exercises in your daily routine:

1. Daily Check-ins: Schedule daily times to share feelings, thoughts, and experiences.

2. Gratitude Journal: Keep a shared journal where you write things you appreciate about each other.

3. Mindful Listening: Practice having conversations where the only goal is to understand your partner.

Reflect on these questions:

1. How often do you practice mindfulness in your relationship?

2. Can you identify an area where you could improve your partner's mindfulness?

3. How can these mindful practices deepen your connection with your partner?

....

....

....

....

....

....

....

....

....

....

....

....

....

....

....

....

....

....

....

....

....

....

7.19 Practice 19: Cultivating Compassion in Your Relationship

Relationships can bring immense joy and fulfillment, but can also present challenges. Effective communication is a crucial element in any relationship, but according to relationship expert John M. Gottman, Ph.D., emotional intelligence is equally essential. This is where compassion, a key component of emotional intelligence, plays a vital role.

Compassion is a deep sympathy for another's suffering with a desire to alleviate their pain. In a relationship, being compassionate means noticing when your partner is going through a hard time and offering kindness as they navigate their challenges.

Considering Abraham Maslow's hierarchy of needs, we all have four fundamental needs after our necessities are met—attention, affection, appreciation, and acceptance. Here are ways to practice compassion in your relationship concerning these four aspects.

7.19.1 Attention
Every individual yearns to be seen, heard, and acknowledged.

7.19.1.1 Listen with Intention

Remove distractions and focus fully on your partner. Listen with your heart rather than your mind and avoid interrupting them.

7.19.2 Affection
Everyone requires a certain amount of affection, even those who aren't overly demonstrative.

7.19.2.1 Be Kind to Your Speech

It's not just what you say, but how you say it. Express your thoughts and feelings with love and kindness.

7.19.3 Appreciation
Everyone, especially loved ones, desires to be valued and appreciated.

7.19.3.1 Nurture the Friendship and Your Relationship

Successful relationships are rooted in mutual respect and enjoyment of each other's company. Spend time discussing shared experiences and support each other's dreams and ambitions.

7.19.4 Acceptance
Everyone wants to be accepted for who they are in their relationships and daily lives.

7.19.4.1 Create a Safe Space for Your Partner to Be Themselves

Create a secure environment for your partner to be genuine. Express your love for them, reassuring them that they are wonderful just the way they are.

There may be times when maintaining compassion in your relationship is difficult. It requires a degree of self-awareness that can sometimes seem overwhelming. However, a moment of self-awareness can help shift your focus from blame to compassion. Instead of dwelling on the negatives, concentrate on the positives. From there, you and your partner can work together to create loving and mindful solutions.

Try implementing these exercises in your daily routine:

1. Compassionate Listening: Set aside specific times each day to listen to each other without distraction.

2. Expressing Affection: Regularly express your love for your partner through both words and actions.

3. Appreciation Notes: Leave small notes or messages of appreciation for your partner to find.

4. Embrace Authenticity: Encourage open and honest conversation, allowing each other to be vulnerable and authentic.

Reflect on these questions:

1. How often do you practice compassion in your relationship?

2. Can you identify a recent situation where you could have been more compassionate?

3. How can these exercises enhance the level of compassion in your relationship?

....

....

....

....

....

....

....

....

....

....

....
....
....
....
....
....
....
....
....
....
....
....
....
....
....

7.20 Practice 20: Show Your Partner Care Through Actions and Words

"Actions speak louder than words", an old adage that mirrors some people's preference for tangible signs of affection over the words "I love you". This is their "love language". Doing something for them might be more appreciated than an occasional gift.

To show your care, make their favorite meal, a gesture of warmth and care. Offer a hug, a physical symbol of affection, but always remember to respect their boundaries. Remember important dates, a sign of respect and care. Praise your loved one on social media, enhancing their sense of appreciation. Create a handmade item, a tangible demonstration of your effort and affection. Lastly, let them pick the movie, a small compromise showing your support.

But please remember words. A text message, a phone call, a postcard, a love letter, a post-it note, or a meme can do a lot to express your feelings.

If you can't be together, there are still ways to show your care. Send a care package, set up a video chat, plan a visit, watch a movie together virtually, send a comfort item or a special gift for no reason.

Exercises:

1. Prepare a surprise dinner with your partner's favorite dish.

2. Remember and celebrate an important date for your partner.

3. Create a social media post praising your partner.

Questions:

1. What are your partner's favorite dishes?

2. Do you know the significant dates for your partner?

3. Do you know what kind of recognition your partner appreciates the most on social media?

....

....

....

....

....

....

....

....

....

....

....

....

....

....

....

....

....

....

....

....

....

....

....

....

7.21 Practice 21: How to Support Your Partner

In relationships, the perfect balance of feminine and masculine energy creates a true connection and sparks of passion. Supporting the partner requires effort, understanding when to step in and when to give space. Verbally express your support, creating a secure environment. Show confidence in your partner and use specific and detailed words to motivate them.

Exercises:

1. Make a list of motivational phrases to use in moments of stress.

2. Plan a surprise activity that your partner enjoys.

3. Write a letter to your partner expressing your admiration and belief in them.

Questions:

1. How does your partner like to be supported during stressful times?

2. What specific words of affirmation resonate most with your partner?

3. What actions can you take to show your support to your partner?

....

....

....

....

....

....

....

....

....

....

....

....

....

....

....

....

....

....

....

....

....

....

....

7.22 Practice 22: Achieve Harmony Between Respect and Self-Respect

Balancing respect for others with self-respect is a key aspect of maintaining healthy relationships. Sometimes, this can be a difficult balance to achieve, especially when you are dealing with strong personalities or difficult situations.

The acronym **FAST** can help guide you in these interactions, promoting fairness, limiting apologies, sticking to your values, and being truthful. This method can help you maintain self-respect, which is essential for a healthy interaction with others.

F: Fair

1. You should aim to be fair to both yourself and others. It's important to consider both your own and the other person's needs and interests. If you make a mistake, take responsibility; if others do, be ready to forgive. Remember, you're all human.

95

A: No Apologies

2. Avoid over-apologizing, especially when you are not at fault. Excessive apologizing can erode your self-esteem, making you feel as if you're in the wrong when you're not. Ask yourself, "Does this situation require an apology?" and try to keep your apologies for when they are genuinely necessary.

S: Stick to Your Values

3. You should never feel as though you have to compromise your values to appease others. It's essential to remember that you don't have to give up your other commitments and interests to maintain a relationship. Consider your core values before making decisions, and strive to live your life according to these principles.

T: Be Truthful

4. Being honest is usually the best approach. Even small lies can undermine trust. While it may be tempting to lie to avoid conflict or to spare someone's feelings, honesty is often the best policy eventually. Avoid making excuses and lying, as these actions only damage your relationships.

Balancing respect and self-respect can be challenging. The dynamics within a relationship can be complex, and it's not always easy to maintain this balance while sticking to your core values. Using the FAST method can help you to develop the skill of maintaining self-respect in your relationships, improving your ability to assert yourself and maintain balanced, healthy relationships.

Exercises:

1. Reflect on a recent interaction where you could have applied the FAST principle. How would it have changed the situation?

2. Take a day to consciously limit your apologies. How does it affect your interactions with others and your feelings about yourself?

3. Identify a situation where you compromised your values to maintain a relationship. How could you have handled it differently while staying true to your values?

Questions:

1. Can you identify a situation where you were not fair to yourself or others?

2. Do you tend to over-apologize? If so, why do you think you do this?

3. Are there values you've compromised in your relationships? If your answer is yes, what sensations did you feel?

4. Can you think of a situation where you were not truthful? Why did you choose to lie, and how could you have handled it differently?

7.24 Practice 24: Mastering Anger Management in Relationships

Anger, when approached correctly, can have beneficial health impacts. If left unchecked, it can harm your relationships and health. Here are seven concise strategies to help regain control when anger threatens to create tension in your personal or professional life:

1. Pause for Reflection: Before reacting in the heat of the moment, take a deep breath and count to ten to prevent regrettable actions or words.

2. Express Calmly: Once calmed, articulate what upset you in a non-confrontational manner. Use "I" statements to express displeasure, such as, "I feel upset when you don't help me with dinner clean up."

3. Use Humor: Lighten the mood with nice humor. Self-deprecating humor can help manage anger and expectations, but avoid sarcasm, as it may exacerbate tensions.

4. Take Breaks: Short, frequent breaks can help reduce stress levels and prevent overwhelming anger.

5. Exercise: Physical activity can effectively reduce stress and mitigate anger. A walk or run can offer emotional relief.

6. Practice Relaxation Techniques: Utilize yoga, meditation, deep breathing, or visualization to promote calm. A daily mantra like "Take it easy" can also be helpful.

7. Forgive: Cultivate the powerful skill of forgiveness to prevent bitterness or feelings of injustice from dominating your emotional landscape.

Remember, it's perfectly normal to have trouble regulating anger from time to time. If anger continues to be a problem despite these strategies, seek help from a mental health professional.

To reinforce this practice, consider these three exercises:

1. Journaling Exercise: Write down three recent instances when you felt angry. Detail the events, your response, and how you could have handled it better.

2. Reflection Exercise: Practice mindful breathing for 5 minutes twice daily. Notice any changes in your feelings and reactions over a week.

3. Role-play Exercise: With a trusted friend, simulate a scenario that angers you. Practice expressing your feelings calmly and constructively.

And, answer these three questions:

1. What common triggers provoke my anger?

2. How can I integrate daily relaxation techniques into my routine?

3. How am I practicing forgiveness, both for myself and others?

....
....
....
....

7.25 Practice 25: Daily Rituals to Strengthen Connection with Your Partner

Living together doesn't always translate to profound understanding or connection. It's not uncommon for couples to realize they've barely connected throughout the day. Including your partner in your resolutions can help deepen your bond. Here are ten simple, daily rituals to help increase intimacy and enhance connection:

1. Actively Respond: Positive responses to your partner's "bids for attention" can contribute to a stronger relationship. Engage when your partner reaches out for attention or discussion.

2. Reunite with Affection: Long separations can stimulate neural systems of former lovers. A warm hug during these reunions can help regulate emotions and mitigate conflict.

3. Establish a Night Routine: After a busy day, the evening can be a prime time to reconnect. Create rituals for bedtime to foster warmth and intimacy.

4. Connect in the Morning: Set aside time in the morning for connection. A quick cuddle or brief conversation about your day can set a positive tone.

5. Reach Out During the Workday: Small gestures during the workday, like a text or email, can convey care and attention.

6. Start Conversations Positively: A nice approach can influence the outcome of a conversation. Consider the difference between accusatory language and a polite request.

7. Show Appreciation: Find something to appreciate about your partner daily and express your gratitude.

8. Prioritize Personal Time: Healthy relationships thrive when both partners maintain individual interests. Devote time each day to focus on your personal well-being.

9. Share Daily Updates: Take at least 10 minutes each day to inform your partner about aspects of your life they might not see or experience.

10. Celebrate Successes: Whether it's a big achievement or a small milestone, share and celebrate each other's successes.

To solidify these daily rituals, try these three exercises:

1. Daily Check-in: Set a dedicated time each day to check in with your partner about their feelings and thoughts.

2. Appreciation Exercise: Each night, share one thing you appreciate about your partner from that day.

3. Success Celebration: Celebrate small and big wins together with a special meal or shared activity.

Reflect on these questions:

1. Which rituals do I find most meaningful for connection?

2. How can I integrate these rituals into my daily routine?

3. What barriers might hinder the successful implementation of these rituals, and how can I overcome them?

....
....
....
....
....
....
....
....
....
....
....
....

7.26 Practice 26: Nurturing Emotional Vulnerability for Deeper Intimacy

Emotional vulnerability is often misunderstood and undervalued in relationships, yet it is crucial for cultivating deeper intimacy. It is the courage to open up, express true feelings, and share personal fears or insecurities with your partner. By doing so, we invite our partner into our inner world, building a stronger bond based on understanding and mutual trust. Here are six key steps to nurture emotional vulnerability in your relationship:

1. Recognize and Acknowledge Emotions: Before expressing your feelings, you must first understand them. Reflect on your emotional state, label your emotions accurately, and accept them without judgment.

2. Cultivate Attentive Listening Skills: When your partner shares their feelings, listen attentively and empathetically without interrupting or judging. Show understanding and validate their emotions.

3. Express Your Feelings Openly: Share your feelings honestly and openly with your partner. Use "I feel..." statements to express your emotions without blaming or criticizing your partner.

4. Embrace Difficult Conversations: Don't shy away from discussing painful or uncomfortable topics. Such conversations can promote understanding and bring you closer.

5. Show Empathy and Compassion: Show understanding and sympathy when your partner expresses vulnerability. Respond with kindness and compassion.

6. Cultivate a Safe Space: Create an atmosphere of trust and safety in your relationship where both you and your partner feel comfortable being emotionally vulnerable.

To solidify this practice, here are three exercises:

1. Emotion Check-In: Set aside a dedicated time each day to share your feelings with each other.

2. Empathy Practice: Whenever your partner shares their feelings, respond with empathy and validation, and switch roles.

3. Vulnerability Challenge: Share something that scares you or makes you feel vulnerable, then discuss your feelings around this sharing.

Reflect on these questions:

1. How comfortable am I with expressing my feelings openly and honestly with my partner?

2. How do I respond when my partner shares their feelings or shows vulnerability?

3. What steps can I take to foster a safer and more accepting environment for emotional vulnerability in our relationship?

....

....

....

....

....

....

....

....

Conclusion

Effective communication is the cornerstone of every successful relationship. It involves more than just talking and listening; it's about expressing one's feelings authentically and profoundly understanding one's partner. Remember, it's not only about hearing the words, but understanding their true meaning and intent. Those who acknowledge this and continuously strive to enhance their communication skills will reap significant benefits. A happy relationship is one characterized by clarity and certainty.

But what communication activities are truly useful, especially for couples with so much to share? We've consulted various experts and have collected their valuable insights. The activities proposed are simple and don't require much time, yet they bring a great return in terms of couple growth and understanding, helping you to focus on crucial skills such as active listening, conflict resolution, and gratitude. By committing to applying these exercises more often, or at least keeping their principles in mind, you'll be able to create more connections and fewer misunderstandings.

It's essential to remember that positivity is the cornerstone of effective communication. According to various studies, it's not so much what you say that matters, but how you express it. The use of negative language can lead to misunderstandings and make the partner feel attacked or accused. Therefore, before speaking, reflect and strive to express yourself in a more positive way.

In conclusion, these are some of the most effective couple communication practices. Their regular application can spare you many hardships and stress, helping you to strengthen your relationship or become stronger as a couple.

Never forget that, beyond fairy tales and romantic novels, successful relationships require effort from both sides. And a large part of this effort concerns communication.

You've learned in this guide that communication in a relationship goes far beyond the simple exchange of information. In fact, the action of making a proposal and receiving a response contributes to strengthening the emotional bond.

You've also learned the importance of developing and maintaining these skills. The most important message to glean from all this is perhaps this: communication in a relationship is not just a matter of style or personal preferences, but a set of skills to be learned and practiced.

The journey to building effective communication and a fulfilling relationship can be long and require commitment, but I assure you that it is worth it. I wish you, readers, to reach your goal of building a rewarding and lasting couple relationship. Your dedication and commitment will lead you to a relationship full of understanding, love, and happiness. Have a nice trip!

Made in the USA
Las Vegas, NV
23 October 2024